CW00407228

FASCINATING EARTH

SOUTH AFRICA

NAMIBIA · BOTSWANA

The cliffs of the "Twelve Apostles" tower above one of the most exclusive coastal stretches on the peninsula. Behind lie the top seaside resorts of Camps Bay and Clifton. Distinctive flowers, typical of the region, cover the slopes.

FASCINATING EARTH

SOUTH AFRICA · NAMIBIA · BOTSWANA

The "Arch" is only one of many erosion formations on the Spitzkoppe. This distinctive mountain is often called "Namibia's Matterhorn" and is considered to be a real challenge to climbers.

ABOUT THIS BOOK

"I am of the firm belief that South Africa is the most enchanting place on earth. Naturally I am biased. But considering the natural beauty of the country, the hospitality and the cultural richness of its inhabitants as well as its being a paradise for all forms of wildlife, I remained convinced that we have been blessed with a truly wonderful place to live." Nelson Mandela

Very few regions in this world confront the visitor with such overwhelming and direct contact with nature. In this respect southern Africa is almost unique. Monumental landscapes such as the Sossusvlei sea of sand dunes and the timeless cave art found in Namibian Damaraland, the lily-covered waters of the Okavango Delta in Botswana – along with its sheer incomprehensible wealth of wildlife – thundering Victoria Falls in Zimbabwe, the majestic peaks of the South African Drakensberg Mountains and the archaic ruggedness found in the Namaqua are destined to lodge themselves in the heart of every observer. To comprehend the power of nature and live alongside her is one of the most intense experiences Africa has to offer: coming face-to-face with elephants, being separated by a mere tent from the voices of the savannah after nightfall, witnessing whales at play just off the shore. An understanding of nature enables an understanding of the peoples of southern Africa: the farmers, whose rhythm accompanies the natural rotation of the seasons; the nomads, whose herds follow the rainfall; the bushmen, whose survival is owed, above all else, to their detailed knowledge of the world in which they live.

The truly breathtaking variety of southern Africa is presented here in topics sectioned geographically. The atlas portion of the book enables you quickly to locate the particular spot you wish to visit – with tourist tips provided. The index, found at the end of the book, is intended to combine photo and atlas pages; this portion also contains the internet addresses essential to finding one's way around. This should all prove helpful in your discovery of southern Africa in all its multi-faceted beauty. Nobel laureate Nelson Mandela is quite right: this is one of the most enchanting spots on earth.

The Publisher

The landscape and the lives of animals, plants and human beings in southern Africa are dramatically shaped by water. Large picture: The Victoria Falls have been declared a UNESCO Natural Heritage Site.

CONTENTS

Southern Africa overwhelms its visitors again and again: the beautiful visual symphony of the orange-red Sossusvlei dunes, the green and white lilies in the Katanga Delta and the warm earth tones of carved wooden cult masks. High above the most beautiful mountains, coasts and plains of the continent you will see a very particular and impressive blue – that of the sky.

An attentive Oryx antelope perceives a change in the air over the Namibian dunes. What she senses are the moisture-laden air currents from the Atlantic.
A creature born to the desert knows instinctively that water means survival. A sea of red-gold dunes surrounds the Sossusvlei, where water from the spring rain still remains. In summer, a period mainly devoid of rain, evaporation takes its toll, leaving behind a cracked residue of clay and salt.

NAMIBIA

Though very dry there is surprising variety in the Namibian landscape: sand dunes, granite hills and mountains are formed in even ranks stretching to the horizon. In some places the landscape is softly rounded and tranquil, covered with golden shimmering grassland; in others it is wild and rough, with bare jagged cliffs, thorny scrubland and quiver trees. The attraction of this somewhat unconventional stretch of southwestern Africa is perhaps the seeming endlessness of the land and the clear cloudless sky above.

Thousands of tiny seals push and shove at Cape Cross, along the Namibian "Skeleton Coast". The coast owes its bizarre name to the many shipwrecks – death was the fate of many an unfortunate sailor whose ship dared to brave the waters here.

The Skeleton Coast

There is no rainfall along the Namibian coast. The Benguela Current brings icy cold seawater from the South Pole down to the equator, cooling the westerly winds that cross from the sea, reducing their ability to hold moisture and resulting in a lack of rainfall. Only the fog banks drifting in from the sea provide plant life and animals with much-needed moisture. For this reason the Namibian Desert is one of the driest spots on earth. Seafarers unlucky enough to be stranded on these shores by the devilish currents here had almost no chance of survival. Dying of thirst, their bodies fell prey to lions or hyenas. Today, the "Skeleton Coast", as the northern portion of the Namibian Desert is known, is a nature preserve. Desert elephants, "singing dunes", the battered remains of sunken ships and the age-old *Welwitschia mirabilis* plant are its main attractions.

Steep gorges, strange bare circles in the grass and the Kunene waterfalls characterize the barren landscape of the Kaokoveld, where the Himba live a nomadic life with their cattle.

Kaokoveld

Kaokoveld in northwestern Namibia is one of the most ancient regions in all of southern Africa. Acacia, thorn bushes and baobabs comprise the vegetation here, and, following the rainy period, a golden grass flourishes. The Himba, a people who have crossed and re-crossed this rugged mountainous landscape with their cattle for centuries, following the changes of seasons, relied on and always found protection and sustenance in Kaokoveld. Now, however, the Namibian government's plans to erect a power plant upon the Epupa Falls of the Kunene are threatening the traditional life of this nomadic people. Roads would be paved, the sacred resting places of their ancestors would disappear beneath a gigantic reservoir and many Himba would come in contact with the disastrous effects of alcohol and other devastating side effects of modern civilization.

Hairstyles reveal one's social status: young girls weave their braids to stand out and project forward. Marriageable young women allow their braids to hang over their faces, while wives shave the hairline above the forehead.

THE HIMBA

During the 16th century the Himba, a nomadic, cattle-rearing people, wandered from the northeast to the southwest of Africa along with other groups of the Herero people. It is commonly believed that the Himba remained in Kaokoveld while the other Herero stayed on, or took refuge in the mountainous wilderness to escape the plundering raids of the Nama. The majority of the Himba have succeeded in preserving their traditional lifestyle until the present day: true nomads, they wander with their herds, erecting temporary settlements with hive-like huts constructed from woven reeds and covered with a mixture of clay and dung. An essential element of every settlement is the eternal, sacred fire, which is tended by the daughter of the tribal chief. There is also the holy tree, from which, according to legend, cattle first come to the Himba. Both men and women wear a loincloth of leather and hide; their bodies are protected from the sun, insects and the drying effects of the wind with the help of a reddish paste. Their only ornaments are iron, strips of leather and seashells. Most Himba hold fast to their traditions, even if, on occasion, in places like Opuwo, they seem to be people from another time. The main threats to this unique culture are alcohol and the frightening spread of Aids.

In bountiful Ovamboland fruit, grain and vegetables flourish, and the fishermen are blessed with generous catches from the numerous rivers and tributaries. Farmers offer their produce at the markets of Oshakati and Ondangwa.

Ovamboland

The former homeland of the Ovambo, Namibia's statistically largest ethnic group, lies between the Etosha National Park and the border with Angola. Countless rivers stream down from the Angolan highlands to the south to replenish this arid region. Almost half of the Namibian population lives crowded together on a mere six per cent of the available land space. Clay yards surrounded by wooden stockade fences and markets form the typical image of life in this part of Africa. Yet it is the dismal settlements around the administrative areas of Oshakati and Ondangwa that provide the true picture of Ovamboland: its high unemployment and miserable living conditions are the major problems of the area. The majority of men, as well as many women, work on farms, in mines and in factories in central Namibia.

The queen of the beasts has seized upon a kudu calf and sent the steppe zebra into wild flight. Now, the lions are satiated and lethargic, allowing the gazelles and zebras a respite: for the moment they have nothing to fear.

Etosha National Park

An area of some 21,000 sq km (8,100 sq miles), Etosha National Park is a UNESCO World Heritage Site offering a protected environment to innumerable wild animals. Elephants, which had almost become extinct, have proliferated to such an extent that there is now a problem of overpopulation; the numbers of rhinos are also increasing. Cheetahs, lions, leopards and hyenas, as well as bat-eared foxes and jackals, are able to satisfy their hunger thanks to the huge grazing herds of antelope, gazelle, zebra and giraffe that abound. The multitude of bird life that is to be found here is also fascinating, from the strange marabous to the distinctive tokos. Following the rainy period even flamingos make an appearance. Three comfortable lodges provide a perfect base for visitors to explore the park, unaccompanied, between sunrise and sunset.

Numerous tributaries cover the narrow Caprivi Strip like a net. Its wetlands and dry savannah provide a home for a multitude of animals and plant life, including the scarlet jay and the water lily.

The Caprivi Strip

Namibia came into possession of the Caprivi Strip – an apron of land ranging from 32 and 90 km (20 and 56 miles) in width and stretching 460 km (286 miles) eastwards – during a land swap between Botswana and Angola. The German chancellor of the time, Graf Leo von Caprivi, gave Zanzibar to the British in 1890. In return he received Helgoland and the strip of land that now bears his name – it was intended to link German South-West Africa with other colonies in the east. Today, the Strip is populated by some 40,000 inhabitants. The west is the home of the bushmen or, more correctly, the San, while various Bantu peoples live in the east. They are known as Caprivians and live mainly from fishing, cattle breeding and working the land. The animals of the region are those of the dry savannah, along with hippos, crocodiles and sitatunga or marsh buck.

In arid Damaraland, this strange rock formation known as the "organ pipes" seems to have been thrust up from the bowels of the earth. The Damara themselves are among the most enigmatic and mysterious peoples in all of southern Africa.

Damaraland

Damaraland is one of the few regions in central Namibia in which black smallholders still work the land and breed cattle. The Damara also manage several tourist camps, for example at Spitzkoppe, and serve as guides to the breathtaking natural wonders and cave art of their native land. Wind and water, working together, are the forces that brought forth these stone wonders, although their origin lies thousands of millennia in the past. Take the "organ pipes", for example: they are the result of the stone being penetrated by flowing lava and then becoming ossified. The surrounding stone has eroded to expose the hard basalt columns. The so-called Vingerclip in the Ugab Valley is the relic of a mighty cliff face which once ran along the entire length of the river, channelling its flow. At the foot is Vingerklip Lodge, certainly one of the very best to be found in Namibia.

Among the most famous examples of cave art in Namibia is the *Lion with the Crooked Tail*, the tip of which is adorned with a paw print. Thousands of examples of this art form are to be found in Twyfelfontein (Damaraland).

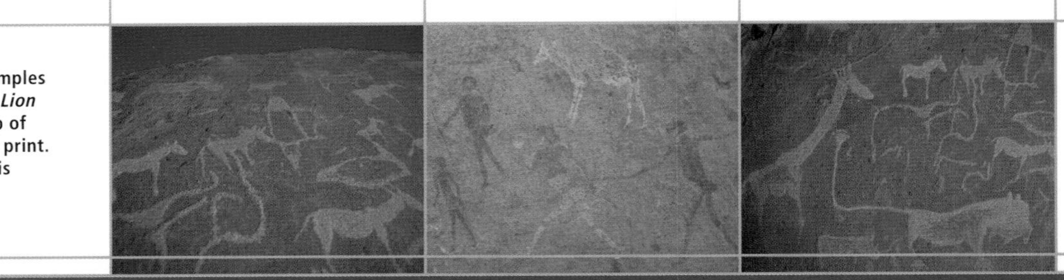

Brandberg

The massive cliff face of Brandberg in north-central Namibia rears up some 2,000 m (6,562 ft) from the coastal plain. Here numerous examples of early Namibian art were discovered in almost inaccessible caves. In nearly every instance hunting scenes are portrayed, and judging by the depictions, game must have been much more abundant than it is today. Humans appear on the walls of caves much less frequently. One exceptional case is the "White Lady", found in the Tsisab Gorge at Brandberg. Clearly visible is a person, carrying a bow and arrow and accompanied by hunters, whose lower limbs and abdomen have been painted white. The artists are still the subject of intense speculation. The most likely hypothesis is that they were the historical ancestors of the so-called bushmen, or the San, as this nomadic people are known today in Namibia.

German cemeteries dating from the colonial period dot the Namibian landscape. One of the bitterest battles of this epoch took place at Waterberg. Those who fell have never been counted.

Waterberg

Central Namibia's "Table Mountain", a massive flat-topped mountain in the northwest of the country stretching up to 50 km (31 miles) in length, is an imposing landmark and also a unique biotope. Its porous stone allows rainwater to seep through only to pour out again along its flanks. It is for this reason that farming land at Waterberg was highly prized during the German colonial period. The Herero uprising started here with an attack on an outback farm and a police outpost. Lieutenant General von Trotha put down the rebellion on August 10, 1904. The so-called "Battle of Waterberg" ended with the Herero being forced out into the Omaheke Desert, with no possibility of return. The actual numbers who perished either from hunger or thirst, or simply of their wounds, is a matter of much debate, and may have been tens of thousands.

It is claimed that the garb of missionaries' wives served as a model for the dress of Herero women today – though the elegant and artful headdresses may recall something other than a traditional mode of dress, they may symbolize the horns of cattle.

THE HERERO

The Herero are regarded as the largest group of Bantu-speaking peoples in north-eastern Namibia, although sparse settlements are also to be found in Kaokoveld. As a cattle-breeding, nomadic people they soon came into conflict with the Nama, a people living mainly in the southern regions. Traditionally the Herero are viewed as comprising three principal groups: the Gobabis Herero or Mbanderu, the Herero of Okahandja (sometimes referred to as the "Maharero People") and the Omaruru Herero. Under the influence of missionaries and pressure from the administration most have become settled. Originally numbering some 80,000 people, the Herero attempted to negotiate with Governor Leutwein for expanded civil rights after their land was seized. When this failed, however, chieftain Samuel Maharero called for a revolt, which ended in the Battle of Waterberg. The majority of the Herero were killed, although some escaped to Botswana; the German administration counted only 15,000 survivors. In view of these events, the traditional garb of the Herero – apparently modelled on colonial styles of dress – seems strange. On special occasions the women appear in distinctive dresses, the men in fanciful, even bizarre, uniforms. Today, the Herero make up the third largest ethnic group in Namibia.

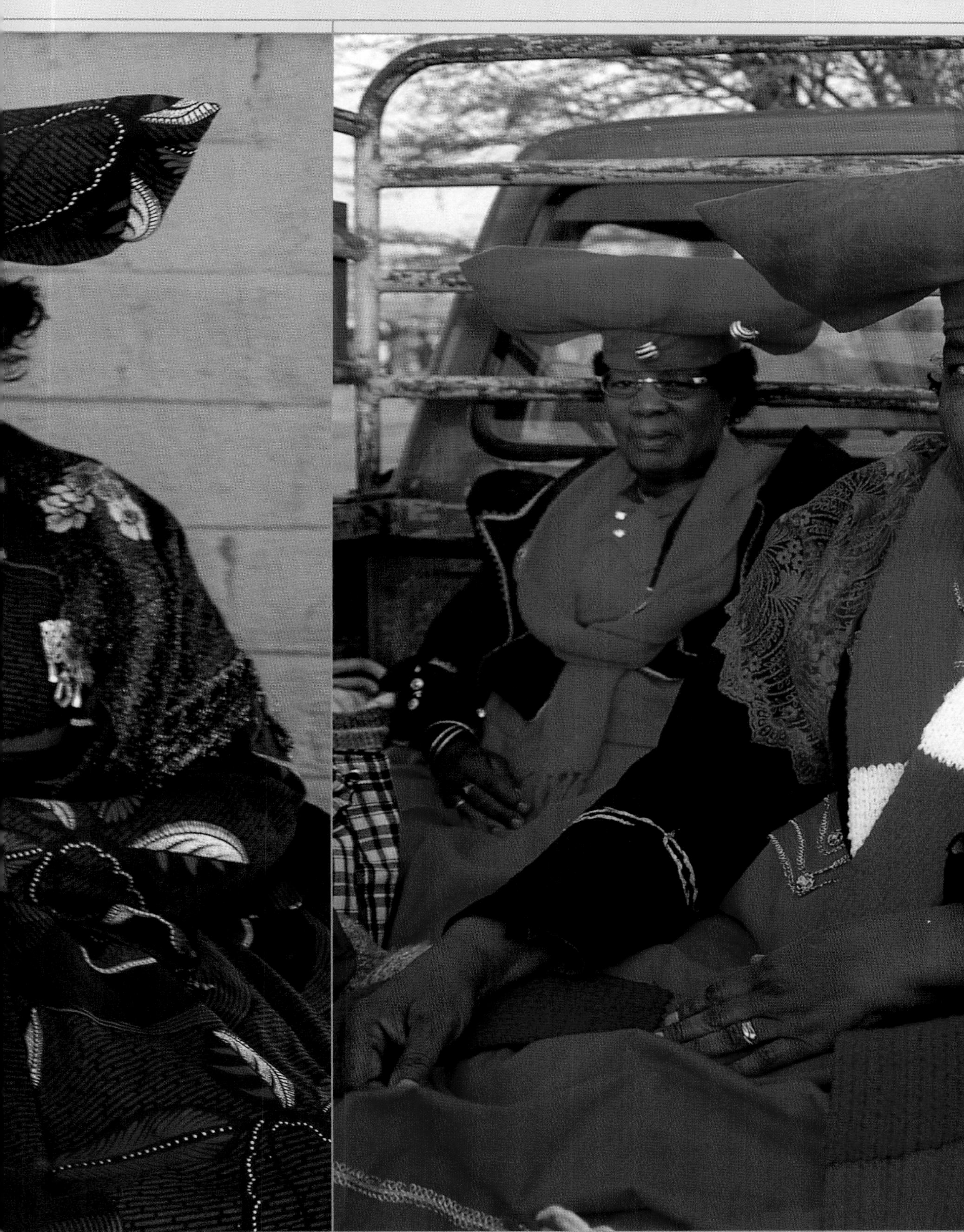

Rocks eroded into unusual and bizarre shapes surprise visitors to Spitzkoppe, from jagged "sculptures" to perfectly rounded spheres. Cave drawings, such as those found east of Spitzkoppe, testify to the early settlement of the area.

Spitzkoppe

The peaks of the Great and Little Spitzkoppe (1,584 m/ 5,197 ft) look like two pointed hats towering skywards. Rainfall over these two isolated peaks is much higher than that over the entire high plateau. The result is that this region is considerably more fertile than the thorn-bush savannah that surrounds it. Amid blocks of granite blooms the botterboom, an African relative of the stonecrop or familiar house leek. Following rainfall the dry, unassuming nodes of the plant yield brilliant yellow blossoms. Cave drawings, such as those found in the hollow known as "Bushman's Paradise" just east of the Great Spitzkoppe, prove that these mountains have served hunters as camp and observation areas since time began. From these elevated sites they were able to enjoy an unobstructed view of grazing herds all across the surrounding plain.

The Erongo Range is a fantasy world of reddish granite and gigantic stone marbles. Rock paintings depict hunters, armed with bows and arrows, tracking buffaloes and elephants.

The Erongo Mountain Range

The Erongo Range is a part of the same great bordering ledge which runs from the central Namibian highlands down to the Namibian Desert. Its peaks, some of which soar to over 2,330 m (7,645 ft), at first seem unspectacular. Its magic becomes evident only within the rocky, broken gorges and the narrow ravines with the bizarre, spell-binding creations wrought by erosion: here an elephant rears its trunk high above a rocky cliff; at another spot a group of buffaloes seems to meet for consultation. Following the rainy season lakes shimmer in stony dips and hollows and lure wildlife to their shores. Paintings on cliff walls and in caves, such as those found in the territory of the Ameib Ranch north of Usakos, depict this mountainous wasteland as a fertile oasis where hunters stalk antelope, buffalo – and a white elephant.

An encounter with a desert elephant certainly numbers among the most moving experiences the visitor can hope for: seemingly carefree, these majestic creatures stomp along the dry riverbed to the next water source, which they can sense beneath the sand.

DESERT ELEPHANTS

Are there really such things as desert elephants? This question is the subject of lively debate, and not only in Namibia. These creatures, found in both southern Kaokoveld and Damaraland, are certainly not a separate species of elephant. Instead, they have probably merely evolved over the years, adapting, like the rhinoceros, to the prevailing conditions in order to deal with and survive in the harsh desert. They can endure two full days without water. Their migration routes run along the dry riverbeds leading westwards from Damaraland and Kaokoveld, often as far as the Atlantic coast and back again. Here, they find grass as well as various leaf-bearing trees, including an occasional mopane, whose bitter-tasting leaves the elephants seem to enjoy particularly. They are able to smell sources of subterranean water and then dig their way to it. Fresh vegetation is not exactly profuse, and these "desert elephants" are consequently somewhat smaller in stature than their counterparts in the Etosha National Park. Since they are not accustomed to contact with humans, they can be aggressive, and it seems that hardly a year goes by without some kind of incident, sometimes fatal. Elephants are particularly prevalent near the Palmwag Lodge and in the bed of the Hoanib River.

In Swakopmund, time seems to stand still. Wilhelminian architecture under African palm trees, swarms of flamingo against a backdrop of North Sea-style lighthouses – these are the contrasts that make the town so endearing.

Swakopmund

At first glance Swakopmund looks like a toy town. Along wide streets, funny little houses painted in pastel shades are set in rows – here, some Art Nouveau, there some Neo-Classicism or even a half-timbered house or two. The width of the streets was determined by the major means of transport in German South-West Africa: the ox-cart drawn by pairs of beasts. The streets are wide because these wagons had to be able to turn full circle.

The grand era of this port town did not last long as it lies on a stretch of coastline that was considered too flat. However, after years of neglect tourism has rejuvenated Swakopmund. Namibians and foreign tourists alike enjoy the nostalgic surroundings and the gourmet fish restaurants, and should the fog close in, an excursion of a few miles to the Namibian Desert will magically summon a brilliant sunny day.

Pure luxury, excellent cuisine, attentive service and an entertaining program of sightseeing all help to sweeten the journey with the Desert Express.

THE DESERT EXPRESS

Namibia's railway network is a bequest of German colonialism and the subsequent period of South African administration. The first railway connection, joining Swakopmund and Windhoek, was inaugurated in 1902; additional lines, such as that via Kolmanskop to Lüderitz Bay or the Northern Line to Grootfontein, followed. The primary purpose of the rail system was to connect the mining areas, for example the Copper Triangle, with the ports, from which ore was transferred by sea. Passengers were of secondary importance, and have remained so; as a consequence Namibian trains cannot hope to compete with travel by bus or private car. Only towards the end of the 1990s was the tourist potential of a railway line that crossed the Namibian Desert recognized. The Desert Express now travels between Windhoek and Swakopmund twice weekly, carrying guests in luxurious two-person compartments, where they are pampered with champagne dinners and fresh oysters. Short stopovers, for example, to pay a visit to the famous lions at the Okapuka guest farm, provide excitement; and at the end of an adventure-packed day, chauffeured jeeps are waiting to convey guests to the Sundowner to experience the sun setting in all its apocalyptic glory over the barren desert wastes.

In Windhoek, the statue of the "Rider" embodies a mindset that seems to say that the past is never really past, although there are many Namibians who would gladly see this rider leave. Today's multi-cultural Windhoek is perhaps best reflected in the glass façades of its shopping malls.

Windhoek

Although Windhoek has grown rapidly since independence, thanks perhaps to its villas and other structures dating from colonial times, it still gives the impression of being a sleepy little provincial town. Late into the 1980s, the government's policy of Apartheid compelled the non-white inhabitants to live in drab, uniform settlements on the outskirts of town. Such a "township" was Katutur. Today, it is predominantly economic considerations that prevent non-white citizens from moving away from the outskirts into the town and villas. Nonetheless, Windhoek remains an important symbol of the successful and, above all, peaceful social transformation of Namibia. The old racial barriers have for the most part been overcome and dismantled, and on the streets and squares of the city you will see clear evidence of a lively multi-cultural society.

Hans-Georg von Hase manages a weaving mill on his farm, Kiripoteb. The carpets he and his employees produce from resilient and durable wool, with their cheerful animal designs and bold patterns, are loved far beyond the borders of Namibia.

LIFE ON THE FARM

Around 44 per cent of Namibia's land area is utilised by commercial farms, either cattle or, in the south, karakul sheep. Most farms belong to whites of either German or South African origin. Many families have lived for generations on the soil; some are able to trace their ancestors back to the original settlers of the colonial period and feel themselves to be as "African" as their indigenous fellow citizens. Depending on the region, an agricultural concern must be between a few thousand and several tens of thousands of hectares in size if a profit is to be made: one head of cattle requires – in this arid climate – between 5 and 20 hectares (12 and 49 acres) of grazing land. Farmers who own vast expanses of land are therefore by no means wealthy. Many of them also offer "room and board", and this gives tourists the unique opportunity to become acquainted at first hand with the hard life on the farms. Excursions, farm tours and hikes allow visitors the opportunity to learn about the land from their hosts and, through closer acquaintance, to form rewarding and lasting friendships. Hans-Georg von Hase runs a guest farm on his large (ca 10,000 hectares/24,710 acres) homestead. A very special visitor attraction is, of course, the weaving mill. His atelier is the birthplace of the famous Kirikara art-wool carpets.

Rocky mountains, stretches of boulders, desert coastlines, sand dunes and their climate-adapted flora are all protected in Namibia's Naukluft Park. One of the most beautiful regions is the majestic Naukluft Mountain Range.

Naukluft Park

With nearly 50,000 sq km (31,070 sq miles), the Naukluft Park is one of the greatest nature preserves on earth. Although the park is comprised of nothing but sand it is by no means monotonous. The sands extend from the blackened gravel regions and the spectacularly eroded solitary hills to the sea of sand that is central Namibia. The Naukluft mountain range, with its rocky peaks rearing some 2,000 m (6,562 ft) upwards, and its deep-cut ravines, provides a very specific kind of ecosystem. Thanks to the abundance of water, a large variety of both animals and plants are able to thrive here: mountain zebras, baboons, jackals and springboks can be seen, as well as bird life such as the eared vulture, sand lark and Namibian lark and other birds. Both types of lark are endemic here and can be found only at the lower rough granite levels.

The vast sea of sand around Sossusvlei appears to be untouched and devoid of life. Yet first impressions can be deceptive; a closer look reveals hundreds of tiny traces left behind by desert creatures, both large and small.

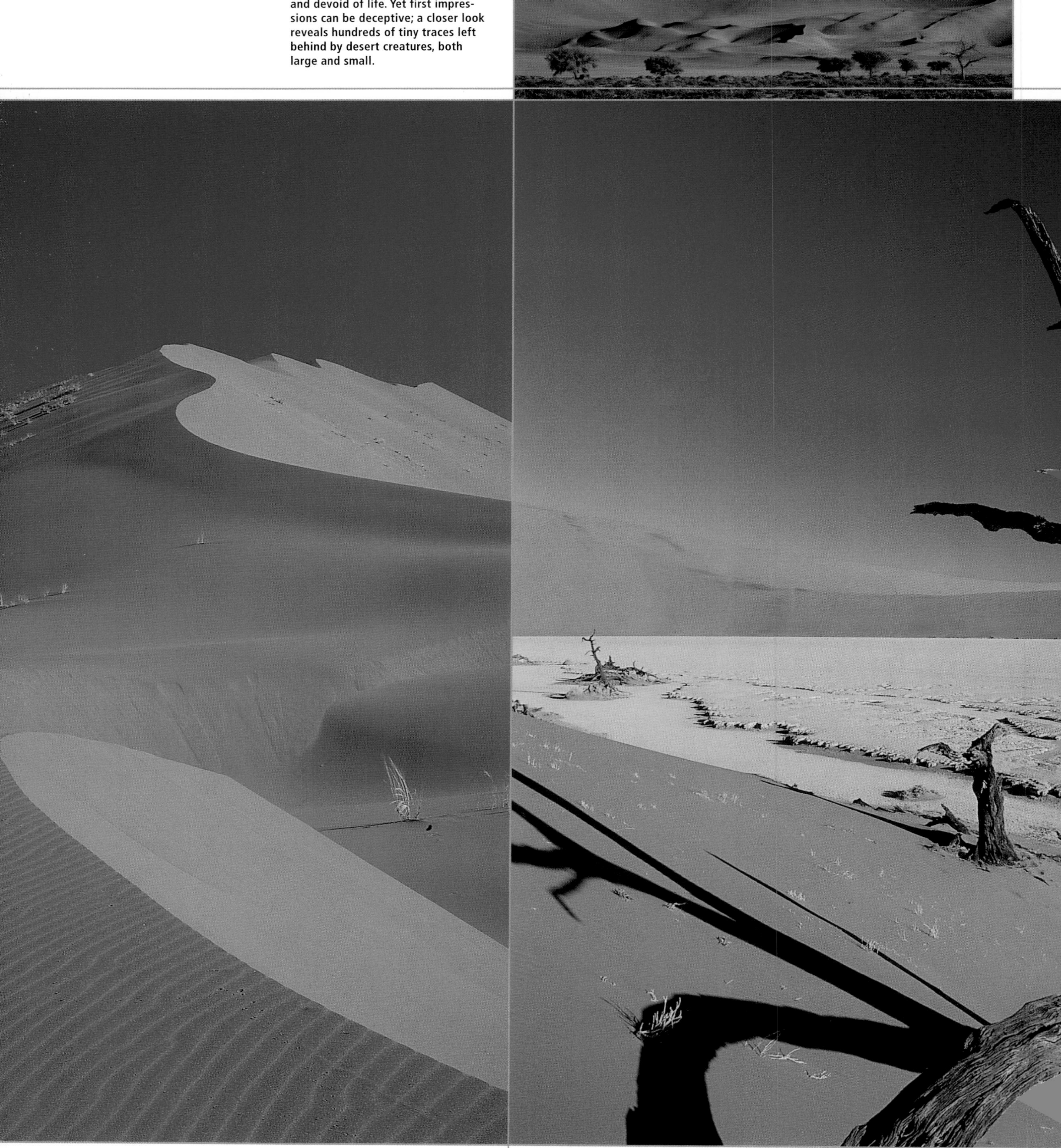

Sossusvlei

It is at Sossusvlei that visitors experience what desert actually means. The vast expanse stretches ahead in almost geometrically perfect waves that appear to touch the horizon. The rich earth tones of the landscape deepen from ochre to orange and red as the day progresses. Tracks criss-cross the flanks of these dunes, silent traces of nocturnal activity in a world that seems so barren and desolate. Smaller desert inhabitants such as the black beetle and scorpion live here, although larger creatures, such as desert rats, jackals and Oryx antelopes are well adapted and able to find sufficient nourishment for their needs. And should the Chauchab River, following a plentiful rainy season, replenish dry riverbeds, then even the desert dips and depressions – which Namibians call vlei – can quench their thirst.

Welwitschia mirabilis is a symbol of the enormous ingenuity and resilience as well as the stubborn persistence demanded of both man and vegetation in order to endure and survive in arid Namibia. Nature makes no exception for the straw flowers (*Helichrysum*, right) either.

WATERED BY FOG AND NOCTURNAL DEW

In the year 1859, the Austrian botanist Friedrich Welwitsch succeeded in identifying and classifying a very strange looking palm-like plant – with leaves that were apparently wilting surrounding an upright flower. Previously unknown, scientists assumed at first that it was some form of plant from an earlier period when the Namibian Desert was not so dry as today, and which had then evolved the special survival tactics necessary to enable it to survive long periods of drought. Welwitsch theorized that during that time *Welwitschia mirabilis* (the plant was named in his memory) developed the means of storing any water it had been able to absorb. When fog banks move inland from the coast, the water condenses on the broad leaves of the plant and then drips to the ground, from where it is absorbed by the roots. Other plants and even animals also utilize this moisture-laden fog. For example, the tenebrio beetle stands on its head, facing the oncoming fog, allowing the moisture to run off its shell into its mouth. The Oryx antelope performs similar acrobatics: it positions itself on the crest of a dune and licks the condensed water off its nostrils. These fog banks are known to move inland for some 100 km (62 miles); in fact there are days when the dunes themselves seem to vanish.

From Lüderitz Bay Adolf Lüderitz set out to colonise southwestern Africa; his portrait (above, right) is still regarded with much esteem today in the tiny port town. Old German traditions now rub shoulders with the modern city and the busy industrial port, sometimes in striking contrast.

Lüderitz

Lüderitz has an eventful past. In the year 1488 Bartolomeu Diaz was the first European to reach this stretch of African coast and he claimed it for the Portuguese Crown. On May 1, 1883, Dr Heinrich Vogelsang set foot on shore, sent by Adolf Lüderitz, a Bremen businessman, to buy land from the Nama people. Chancellor Bismarck's Protectorate Declaration (1884) transformed the settlement into a German colony. At the beginning of the 20th century Lüderitz experienced a diamond boom but sank into oblivion immediately afterwards. The town had a second boom in the 1990s as the country's sole port was returned to Namibia. Today Lüderitz is preparing itself for its new role as host to tourists from far and wide: the old colonial architecture and wild and rugged Southern Atlantic coastline are now attracting increasing numbers of visitors.

The Nama are considered, along with the San, to be the oldest inhabitants of southern Africa. They live chiefly in the south of the country and generally find employment as farm workers and household help.

THE NAMA

The Nama differ in appearance from the other peoples of Namibia: their skin is lighter, their hair less wiry and, with their prominent cheekbones, they have an Asian physiognomy. One of the smaller ethnic groups, they make up about five per cent of Namibia's population. The language of the Nama and the San set them apart from the Bantu-speaking Herero, Ovambo and Caprivians in the north. While the nomadic San moved from place to place, following their prey, the Nama raised cattle and robust, fat-tailed sheep. Their possession of cattle led to ferocious wars with the Herero. Apart from their language, the Nama and San have other cultural similarities. A notable example is their shared fear of the dead. In earlier times, a settlement would be abandoned following a death. The Nama were among the first peoples to come into contact with Christian missionaries, whose influence has been sustained. In 1814, the German missionary Heinrich Schmelen, a member of the London Missionary Society, established the first missionary station in southwestern Africa, in Bethanie. He married a Nama woman and built what is now considered the oldest European dwelling in Namibia. The deep religious feelings of the Nama are evidenced in their extended church services, which leave a singular impression.

The grandeur of Namibia can be appreciated only from an aircraft or via a satellite picture. It is almost inconceivable that in such an apparently endless sandscape, life not only exists, but thrives.

Namibia's South

The central Namibian Desert in the southern portion of the country is a gigantic, little-explored region under strict environmental protection. Visitors are cautioned to travel only on the very fringes: to the dunes surrounding the Sossusvlei; to the equally majestic dune formations found on the edges of the privately-owned Namib Rand Nature Reserve and those at Walvis Bay on the coast running along Sandwich Harbour, a lagoon landscape. In fact, the Namibian Desert is considered one of the most ancient desert regions on earth; in contrast to the Sahara, which was a water-rich savannah some 10,000 years ago. Here the life-giving waters disappeared about three million years ago. Only a few dry riverbeds, mere streams, serve to convey water for a few weeks in the year, providing the sole source of life for the plants and animals that have made their home here.

Shafts of slanting sunlight make the cracked and brittle bark of the quiver trees shimmer gold, highlighting the extraordinary symmetry of the leaves and flowers.

QUIVER TREES

Exquisite and photogenic: the *Aloe dichotoma* or quiver tree was first mentioned as "kokerboom" as early as 1685 in an official communiqué of the Cape Colony Governor, Simon van der Stel. The governor reported that bushmen made arrows from the wood of the tree. Of course, quiver trees have ancient origins and are "documented" upon cave walls where their distinctive shapes are easily recognizable. The plant is endemic to southern Africa and is a true Namibian "survivor" in its given environment: the spongy tissue in the trunk and the branches retain the water needed to endure the dry months. Its bark is as thin as paper; the dark green leaves, which become yellowish with age, are full and fleshy. And when it blossoms in June and July, bees and birds swarm about its crown – the sweet nectar even attracts the occasional baboon. Quiver trees prefer rocky ground and are most often solitary – thus the quiver tree grove found at Keetmanshop in southern Namibia is actually quite uncommon. Silkweaver birds often nest in the crown, giving the impression that the tree is sporting garlands of straw. The Nama traditionally make use of the dead branches and trunk of the quiver trees to keep their water and provisions cool. The roots of the plant are thought to provide a treatment for asthma.

Sand is slowly burying the last traces of the great diamond boom in Kolmanskop. The fortune-hunters of yesterday have long since passed over the horizon. Their bowling alley, hotels, sport hall and elegant villas have been reclaimed by the desert.

Kolmanskop

In 1908, a black African worker found a diamond near the railway station at Kolmanskuppe; his foreman, August Stauch, secured prospecting rights for himself. Soon afterwards, some 20,000 German diamond hunters descended upon the desert areas of Lüderitz Bay, and a smallish town, offering all the conveniences desired by the hard-working men, came into being. For a time the yield from Kolmanskop supplied approximately one fifth of the world's diamonds. But then the glittering, money-spinning river ran dry. Under the terms of the South African Mandate and as a possession of the diamond conglomerate CDM, Kolmanskop was abandoned, and newer finds further southwest at the mouth of the Orange River proved more profitable. Today, Kolmanskop, almost engulfed by sand, has become a very popular tourist attraction.

These are images from the earth's very beginnings: the naked cliff-faces along the Fish River Canyon tell the history in stone of the birth of our planet: surging magma, earthquakes, tectonic shifts, land-folding and the power of erosion.

Fish River Canyon

Fish River Canyon, some 500 m (1,640 ft) deep, came into being about five hundred million years ago as a result of a geological fault. The canyon is one of the largest in the world. It runs from north to south, and along its walls, layer after layer, lies evidence of the earth's history, hewn in stone, in the dark seams of metamorphic rock, probably some one billion years old, and in the black, mostly vertical intrusions of dolerite, which are the result of volcanic activity. The lower portion of the canyon was created by the erosive effects of the Fish River, which meanders its way among cliff spurs and insular stone bluffs. As the waters of the river are held back by the Hardap Dam, it generally carries little water upon this section of its course. Quiver trees and other desert-adapted plants have managed to root on the cliff walls.

An elephant herd reaches a wide tributary in the delta – their thirst is quenched. Seasonal migration of wildlife is typical of this desert area. In the Okavango Delta, which once belonged to a lake that disappeared some 10,000 years ago, annual flooding makes the survival of the abundant plant and animal life here possible. In the middle of the Kalahari Desert, lilies open their tender blooms.

BOTSWANA

Although perhaps 90 per cent of Botswana's land mass consists of desert and salt flats, such as those found in Makgadikgadi or Nxai Pan, the country possesses a fabulous wealth of wildlife. Botswana is one of the few affluent nations in Africa. The most important source of income is mining (nickel, copper, coal), in particular diamond mining. Nevertheless, some 45 per cent of the population work in agriculture. The most profitable branch of the economy is cattle breeding, chiefly for export.

The waters are coming: when the floods of the Okavango reach the delta, the earth sucks up the moisture like a sponge. Hippos and many other mammals rear their young during this period of plentiful water.

The Okavango Delta

Botswana's Okavango Delta is a unique, completely natural biotope in the Kalahari. Its existence is owed to the water coursing down the Cuando River, in the Angolan highlands. Flowing through Namibia and northern Botswana it spreads out across 15,000 sq km (9,321 sq miles) of inland delta, after which it almost runs dry. Following the rainy period, the rivers of the Cuando reach the delta in June, ovewhelming the land. Islands are formed from former high ground, and a lush, green overgrown Garden of Eden emerges from the dry and desolate Kalahari. This river, known in Botswana as the Okavango, provides the sustenance for the huge herds of zebra, gnu or wildebeest, buffalo, antelope and elephant, which are followed by lions, leopards, cheetahs and other beasts of prey. Crocodiles and hippos make their homes in the water channels.

The River Chobe runs along the border between Botswana and Namibia; the woods lining the river's course, as well as the adjacent thorn-bush savannah, are home to huge herds of elephants. But these grey giants are not the only creatures to come to the river to quench their thirst.

Chobe National Park

The Chobe National Park was established in 1968. With an area of around 12,000 sq km (7,457 sq miles), the park contains several contrasting landscapes, from those graced with lush, overgrown river embankments, to patches of tree-rich savannah and stretches of endless dry desert. Along the banks of the Chobe the Savuti wetlands in the southwest of the park teem with animal life. Chobe's true wealth is its elephants, although many environmentalists on the continent tend to view the unbridled proliferation of this species as an ecological problem. The elephants eat everything available and also penetrate national parks to feed, causing widespread destruction. A similar problem is the growing lion population: the more lions there are, the more difficult it is for smaller predators such as cheetahs and bat-eared foxes to survive.

The San people, resident mainly in Botswana and eastern Namibia, are quite small in stature, with prominent cheekbones, a relatively light skin tone and peppercorn hair. Their language includes a variety of clicking sounds.

THE BUSHMEN (SAN): A CULTURE OF MILLENNIA

"This man, who was once heir over all he surveyed, is today master over nothing. He has not the basic right to hunt where and when he would in order not to die of hunger out in the wastes". The author of these lines, Laurens van der Post, has immortalized the culture of the bushmen, or San, as they are properly called; van der Post's work has also succeeded in establishing a worthy memorial to the San people. Yet, as early as the 1950s, when his books first appeared in print, it was evident that the San were doomed to extinction. Today, the state of the some 100,000 San is critical. Alcohol has ruined the lives of those who have come into closer contact with civilization. Prohibitions against hunting force the men to take on menial farm jobs. The situation of the San in Botswana is even more drastic than in Namibia. Nomadic tribes living in the Central Kalahari Game Reserve have been forced from their lands and driven into slum dwellings because it is believed that valuable natural resources exist beneath their lands. In a few hundred years their culture will have died out, the culture of a people with a deeply-felt sense of oneness with, respect for and an intimate familiarity with nature and her ways. At tourist lodges and farms the San have at least found new employment as nature guides.

The Kalahari is far removed from being desolate and devoid of life; between its ribs of sand are fertile dips and depressions where hyenas, meerkats – a type of mongoose – cheetahs and armadillos can find nourishment.

Kalahari

The dunes of the Kalahari run in narrow ribs parallel to each other. These are in fact fossil dunes, whose substratum has long since turned to stone and remains fixed in place. Water can be found seeping to the surface in the depressions between the dunes; its source lies beneath the ground and is connected to the Okavango inland delta. In seasons when the delta is well irrigated, the water extends to the furthest reaches of this network. If the source fails, the water withdraws. This process provides the Kalahari with a relatively generous bounty. In the valleys there are giraffes, Oryx antelopes, zebras and springboks; predators both large and small stalk their game; grass and acacia stabilize the sandy substratum. The beauty of this constant transition from green to dusty brown compares easily with the majesty of the Sossusvlei dunes.

One of the most breathtaking spectacles in all of southern Africa must be the Victoria Falls (Mosi-oa-Tunya). The river flows in the border region between Zimbabwe and Zambia into a crevice just a few metres wide and plummets 110 m (360 ft).

AN EXCURSION TO THE VICTORIA FALLS

In 1855, word of the "thundering fog" was enough to entice the Scottish missionary David Livingstone to travel the Zambezi ever further into the "heart of darkest Africa". At his journey's end he stood before the most spectacular waterfall the African continent has to offer. The falls owe their name to Britain's Queen Victoria. By the beginning of the 20th century the first tourists were on their way to the Victoria Falls. In fact, in 1904, the renowned Victoria Falls Hotel opened its doors. Then, as now, it was the most prestigious place to be. In 1905, the railway bridge over the Zambezi Gorge was inaugurated; today it is a bungee-jumping location. The Victoria Falls are the result of an ongoing process of erosion – the river cuts ever-deeper crevices and gorges. The first waterfalls were about 8 km (5 miles) from their present location, and this development continues year after year. The falls are at their most exciting when the river isn't flowing with an over-abundance of water, because the falls themselves can then be discerned behind the thundering shroud of misty vapour. The constant "rainfall" in the gorge has resulted in the creation of a tropical rainforest, whose vines and blossoms frame enchanting small clearings. The Victoria Falls are recognized as a UNESCO World Heritage Site.

For generations of seafarers and those who sought their fortune on foreign shores, the sight of Table Mountain was symbolic of a successful crossing and of hope for a better future.

South Africa is the most modern and industrially advanced country in Africa. Yet even in the flashy urban canyons of the boomtowns the language of masks is both remembered and understood.

SOUTH AFRICA

Apartheid and its repressive policies are now history; today's South Africa is well on its way towards transforming itself into a modern, multi-cultural society, the most dynamic economic engine on the continent, and a tourist magnet. South Africa brings together untouched, virgin landscapes, national parks rich in vegetation and wildlife, old towns, futuristic urban cityscapes, and wild, rough and rugged coasts, in a successful synthesis of old European and traditional African culture.

Johannesburg's shimmering nightlife and its modern skyline merely display the upside of this throbbing financial and industrial boomtown. The difficult living conditions of most of those on a low income remain well hidden from view.

Johannesburg

No one knows exactly how many people live in the city of Johannesburg. Officially there are two million, yet many more live in the "suburbs"; these, for the most part, in miserable dwellings made of corrugated iron in the former townships and squatter settlements. White South Africans refer to the city simply as "Jo'burg", black Africans as "e'Goli' ("City of Gold"). Johannesburg began to boom in 1886, when gold was discovered at Witwatersrand, and within a few brief years a town, equipped with a school and its own hospital was established. At the beginning of the 20th century some 150,000 white residents were registered inhabitants. Nowadays, the majority of the old mines are unprofitable. Johannesburg has now developed from an old-time gold-mining town into a financial hub, burdened, however, with a serious security problem.

From the Union Buildings on the Meintijeskop Heights (large picture, below) South Africa's parliamentarians may glance down upon their elegant capital and its futuristic downtown area. When the jacaranda trees are in bloom, the city is covered with a veil of deep purple.

Pretoria

South Africa's administrative capital cannot honestly be described as lively, but rather sedate and "proper". It is the seat of parliament, which convenes in the fine, historic Union Buildings, in session bi-annually; the second session is conducted in Cape Town. Pretoria was founded on the historic settlement grounds of the Ndebele in the mid-1900s. It is named after General Pretorius, who defeated the Zulus at the Battle of Blood River. That the new South African government is considering a change of name is not surprising, although the proposed re-naming to "Tshwane" has been met with some resistance. While Pretoria at first glance appears quite modern, there are numerous 19th-century structures from the time of the city's foundation which give the lie to this. One good example is the fanciful and striking Melrose House.

Abstract patterns and bright, contrasting tones are typical and characteristic of the wall paintings, body decoration and traditional clothing of the Ndebele women. In former times they painted with natural, earth pigments; today modern acrylics are mixed with clay to create an effect.

THE NDEBELE

The Ndebele entered their first settlement areas at some point during the 16th century. Under the harsh rule of Apartheid they were allotted the Kwa Ndebele Homeland north of Pretoria and many of the 400,000 Ndebele still live there. Most of the villages, however, are populated solely by women, children and the elderly – the men have to seek work in the industrial areas of the country. Despite the restrictions on their living space and the wrenching apart of the family fabric, traditions such as wall painting and the graphic body art of the Ndebele have been maintained in isolated enclaves. The tradition of façade painting is as ancient as the people itself, with many patterns being passed down from generation to generation; others have arisen in response to the changing times, as abstractions of contemporary artefacts such as the car, television and other modern appliances, or are modified representations of everyday items such as safety razors, or structures around the home, such as a staircase. Each house bears the personal and characteristic "stamp" of its residents, yet the patterns change, being redone or painted over when significant ritual events take place. This is living art amid social change; at the same time they revere and preserve the traditions of the previous generation.

Magnificent palaces, gambling dens... Sun City is the happy hunting ground of the hustler and visitors in search of Las Vegas-style fun under African skies. It is a glitzy money machine with the largest casino on earth and luxury hotels such as the dazzling "Palace" found in the "Lost City".

Sun City

The African answer to Las Vegas, it is no coincidence that Sun City was constructed in 1977 just northwest of Johannesburg in the Republic of Bophuthatswana, a former "homeland" which itself had only just been granted its independence. The laws affecting gambling were far more liberal there than elsewhere, and it soon became a haven for mixed-race couples seeking to escape the rigours and restrictions of life under Apartheid. In 1992 the gambling and hotel complex was expanded further, with the addition of the "Lost City", a sort of Disneyland, which displays the many cultures of Africa. There is a tropical forest equipped with recordings of animal noises, rustles, squawks and roars while a paradisaical "sleepy lagoon" completes this clichéd depiction of the Dark Continent in the grounds of the deluxe Palace Hotel.

The national park in northeastern South Africa offers spectacular natural wonders such as the 92-m (302-ft) Lisbon Falls and the bizarre Bourke's Luck Potholes. A highlight must be the sunset viewed from the observation point of God's Window.

The Blyde River Canyon Nature Reserve

The Blyde River originates at the old gold diggers' settlement of Pilgrim's Rest, from where it flows northwards to merge with the Treur River just before Blyde River Canyon, finally emptying its waters into the Olifants River. After the Grand Canyon in the United States and Namibia's Fish River Canyon, it is the third largest canyon in the world. This fascinating landscape holds great charm for the visitor, thanks not only to the amazing shapes produced by erosion – its main characteristic – but also because of the wide variety of vegetation, from the tropical rainforest to the dry savannah of Lowveld, some 500 m (1,641 ft) above sea level. The Panorama Route along the canyon leads to impressive lookout points such as the Three Rondavels – cliff promontories that have been worn down by erosion to resemble the traditional round huts of the Xhosa.

In Kruger National Park chance encounters with leopards are nothing out of the ordinary. Large herds of zebra and giraffe saunter through the bush, baboons are always on the lookout for something to snack on and hippos dispute and defend their watery territory.

Kruger National Park

Kruger National Park is the most popular tourist destination in South Africa and is an important source of revenue. This nature reserve, established some hundred years ago, is still the largest on the continent; 2,000 km (1,248 miles) of tracks and paved roads make its approximately 20,000 sq km (12,428 sq miles) accessible to the visitor. There are also 15 camp sites, ranging from simple tents to luxury camps. From the thornbush savannah in the north, vegetation becomes progressively denser towards the south: forests of mopane trees, broad, grassy plains and dense acacia woods provide a home for both white and black rhinoceros, elephants, 17 different types of antelope and 1,500 lions. Buffaloes wander through the bush, giraffes nibble on the leaves of the acacias and more than 500 species of bird provide a never-ending concert, music to the ears of those who come to see the wildlife here.

South Africa is a true paradise for bird-lovers: both in the national parks, and elsewhere in the country more than 850 different types of birds have been sighted. Above, from left: Bee-eater, yellow-billed stork, kingfisher, and Mozambique girlitz. Below left, from top to bottom: Bearded vulture, white-tailed eagle, darter, and saddle stork. Large picture: Hornbill.

THE BIRD WORLD OF SOUTH AFRICA

South Africa's birds are often overlooked. Alongside some 850 types in permanent residence there are numerous seasonal guests from Europe. Among the most eye-catching natives are the bearded vulture and the elegant white-tailed eagle, the darter and the saddle stork, all of which prefer wetlands. A good eye is needed to catch sight of little fellows such as the bee-eater, kingfisher and the Mozambique girlitz, which is related to the canary. Ground-living species include the hornbill, which, owing to its average four-kilogram body weight is scarcely able to lift itself into the air. Hornbills build their nests chiefly in baobabs and the yellow-billed stork (*Mycteria ibis*) stirs the water with its foot to flush out prey. It is an understatement to say that the wildlife attractions of the country are rich and varied when in fact they can be expressed only in superlatives: here are to be found the largest land-going mammals (elephant), the tallest of the tall (giraffe), the most fleet-footed (cheetah), the smallest (Etruscan shrew mouse), the largest bird (ostrich), the largest flying bird (giant bustard) as well as the largest of all turtles (the leatherback turtle). And just off the coasts, in the south particularly, the largest animal believed ever to have lived on earth, the blue whale, plays in the spray.

A healing woman from the Kingdom of Swaziland displays her most essential working utensils. As with many other Swazi traditions, the warrior dress has been preserved. The mountainous landscape is home to the shy desert lynx.

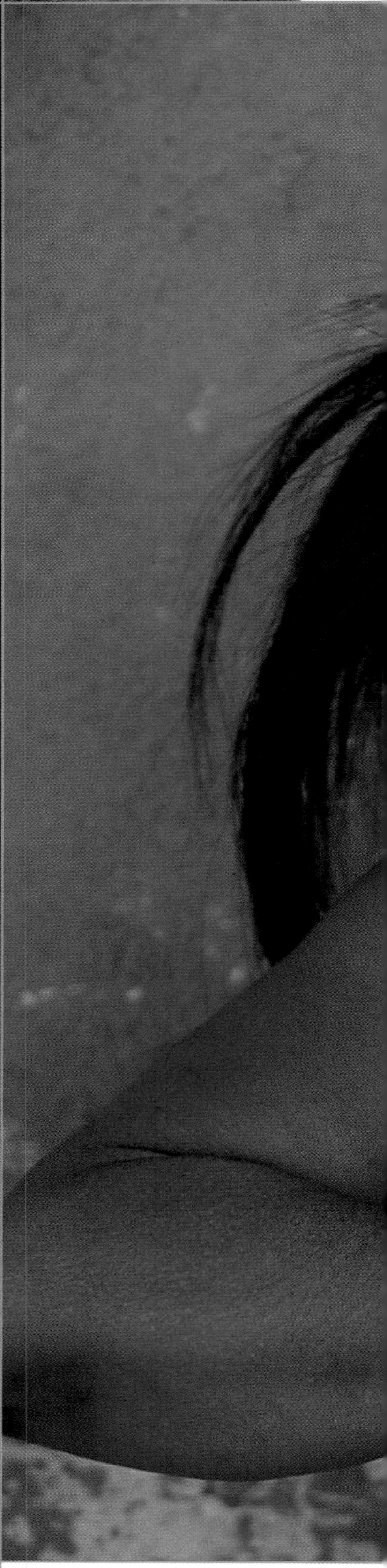

Swaziland

Swaziland is an independent kingdom in the northeast of the country and is ruled as a parliamentary monarchy by King Mswati III. Covering an area of some 17,364 sq km (10,790 sq miles), Swaziland is smaller than Kruger National Park. Its geographic regions stretch from Lowveld in the east, with its dry savannah some 300 m (984 ft) above sea level, to Middleveld, the upper midlands, with its green and lush hills, to the western mountain region at a height of 1,862 m (6,109 ft), covered by dense forests. Swaziland's charms are its magnificent landscape and traditional villages. Plants and animal life are protected in several national parks, but it is the prolific bird life which truly stands out here. The capital of Swaziland, Mbabane, is scarcely more than a provincial hamlet, although it does have a lively little market.

The game reserves of Hluhluwe (pronounced: "shlu-shlu-we") and Umfolozi are numbered amongst the oldest reserves in all of Africa. They are linked to each other by an access road allowing the visitor to move about within one large game park.

You can find both white rhino (*Ceratotherium simum*, above) and black rhino (*Diceros bicornis*) here. Spreading acacia trees shade one of the many small-lakes where, morning and evening, large animal herds come to refresh themselves.

The Hluhluwe-Umfolozi Game Park

These two comparatively small game reserves north of Durban, Hluhluwe and Umfolozi, were established as early as 1895. Together they encompass barely 1,000 sq km (620 sq miles) of hills and valleys, for the most part covered by dense undergrowth and watered by streams large and small. Buffaloes, antelopes, elephants and zebras share these close quarters with lions, leopards and a variety of rare domestic bird life. It is the ideal spot for observing the elegant nyalas, the bat-eared fox and the white rhino, whose number at the beginning of the 20th century was estimated at just 20, teetering dangerously close to extinction. Both black and white rhinos have square-shaped lips, ideal for grazing on grass, and two horns. In addition to the tracks for vehicles, several well-marked hiking paths run through the parks.

Had mining companies prevailed in achieving their goals, neither crocodiles nor hippos would exist today along Lake St Lucia. Yet, thanks to the involvement of environmental action groups this unique biosphere has become a UNESCO World Heritage Site.

The Greater St Lucia Wetland Park

At the heart of the 2,500-sq km (1,554 sq miles) national park on the northeastern coast of KwaZulu-Natal is Lake St Lucia, with an area of 380 sq km (236 sq miles), separated from the Indian Ocean by a girdle of dunes. The lake is fed by several rivers and at high tides it also receives seawater. The low salt content of the water attracts a great number of bird species, which feed well in the shallow brackish water. Flamingos, pelicans, waders, darters and tasselled cranes make their way to the lake and meet along the shoreline, which is also under environmental protection. Hippos wallow in the water and crocodiles lie in wait amid the mangrove swamps. Further inland, buffalo, antelope and rhino make their way across the savannah.The coral reefs found just off the coast are home to a variety of marine life.

The Zulus met the European colonists with fierce resistance and went on to conquer parts of modern Zimbabwe. Today, dances performed in traditional dress are a popular attraction for tourists from Europe and other parts of the world.

THE ZULUS

Ten million strong, the Zulus comprise the largest ethnic group in South Africa; they live mainly in the KwaZulu-Natal region and in Johannesburg. At the beginning of the 19th century their king, Shaka, led them into a war, in the course of which they conquered large tracts of southern Africa, not only subjugating the peoples, but also banishing or killing them. As king, Shaka was the head of a hierarchically organized military state. In 1828, he was murdered by his half-brother Dingane, who subsequently attempted to stem the advance of the Boers into those parts of South Africa not yet colonized – but to no avail. In the legendary Battle of Blood River (1838) the Boer general Pretorius succeeded in vanquishing an army of some 12,500 Zulu warriors; Pretorius himself had a mere 500 men under his command. The battle was a disaster for the Zulus; they lost over 3,000 men. In KwaZulu-Natal several Zulu kraals such as "Shakaland" – actually newly-erected for tourists – recall the martial history and the rich traditions of the Zulu people. The political opponents of the Zulu are the Xhosa. The animosity runs so deep that in 1994 Zulu chief Buthelezi was willing to risk a civil war to prevent the formation of a government by the Xhosa-dominated ANC. Today, the Zulu party, Inkatha, leads the opposition.

Recalling the time of the Great Trek: a defensive ring of covered wagons calls to mind the Battle of Blood River; the town hall of Pietermaritzburg with its decorative clock tower was the site of the first "raadsaals" (parliamentary council) of the Boer Republic of Natal.

Pietermaritzburg

The "voortrekkers" – those Boers who, travelling only in covered wagons, advanced ever further northwards in their vain attempt to distance themselves from English colonial rule – are the object of particular admiration in Pietermaritzburg. It was not far from here that the victorious Battle of Blood River (1838) against the Zulus took place. Yet the era of the Natal Republic was short-lived. In 1843, the English annexed the area and placed it under colonial administration. Most Boers then marched on. Historical structures, such as the town hall with its 47-m (154-ft) clock tower, Tatham Gallery and the Old Colonial Building, are dotted about the town. Boer relics are to be found in the Voortrekker Museum. The "City of Flowers" is fully entitled to its name: spacious parks and the purple blossoms of the jacaranda give it a breezy air.

A tour along the legendary "Golden Mile" beachfront, past Durban's modern cityscape, in a rickshaw pulled by a man in a fearsome warlike headdress is an opportunity not to be missed.

Durban

Durban is South Africa's third largest city, an important industrial and financial area equipped with a modern port, but best known as a place for leisure and sport. This metropolis on the Indian Ocean is South Africa's secret Asian capital – some 400,000 Indians live here – their temples, restaurants and markets give the town an oriental air. Durban Bay was discovered as early as 1497 by Vasco da Gama. In the mid-19th century Durban developed into a flourishing market for the sugar industry. Workers were brought from India as field hands. Those early immigrants included Gandhi, the Father of Indian Independence, who arrived in 1883. Sightseeing highlights include the beachfront with the city's skyline, the "Golden Mile", the Indian Quarter with its lively Victoria Market and the well-preserved colonial structures in the central part of the city.

Indian graffiti on African soil: at Victoria Market everyone feels at home. One unconventional building is the Hare Krishna "Temple of Understanding" (above and below left), located in a suburb of Durban.

INDIANS IN DURBAN

When, in the 19th century, the area around Durban was blessed with a sugar boom, plantation owners found themselves at their wits' end in their search for workers. The proud Zulus refused to demean themselves with such work and, consequently, Indian workers were recruited. For members of the lower castes, the opportunity was particularly tempting, since it offered the possibility of climbing the social ladder in a country where the caste system was unknown. There was, nevertheless, very strict segregation of the races. Mohandas Gandhi (his later title of "mahatma atman" means "great soul") worked as a lawyer. In 1893, having seated himself in a railway compartment reserved for whites, he was unceremoniously thrown off the train by an irate conductor at Pietermaritzburg. One year later he founded the Natal Indian Congress, which aimed to advance the rights of Indians. In 1914, the Indian community was granted privileges that were withheld from the black Africans. Today, some three per cent of the population are of Indian extraction. Most are of the Hindu faith – their temples and rituals make a distinct and rich contribution to the cultural diversity of the country. Many live in the larger Durban area as well as in almost all the large South African towns and cities.

The waters around Durban are considered one of the best spots on the globe to snap a photo of the notorious Great White Shark. If divers' tales can be believed, gigantic sharks of up to 20 m (66 ft) in length have been sighted.

THE GREAT WHITE

The earliest descendants of today's sharks lived four hundred million years ago. While they have hardly changed since then, their environment certainly has. South Africa's coasts, particularly the stretches along Durban and Cape Town, are known for the presence of the Great Whites. The largest shark ever spotted is said to have been 6.6 m (22 ft) long and 3,285 kg (7,243 lb). Today's specimens fall considerably short of these statistics. Based on the frequency of encounters, actual attacks occur only seldom. Along the entire coast, there are between five and seven attacks per year, at least one of which normally ends fatally. However, an increase in attacks has been registered. The reason for this, according to some, lies in the extremely strict protective regulations introduced in 1991, which have allowed the creatures to multiply. Others maintain that it is the tourist agencies that are responsible: in order to lure the sharks closer to the shore, they dump a mixture of blood, oil and fish remains into the water. While this works, in that it does indeed brings the sharks closer to land, it also conditions them to associate human beings with food. Surfers are common targets because their surfboards resemble seals when viewed from beneath, and seals head the menu of the hungry shark.

The Drakensberg Mountains, soaring to 3,000 m (9,843 ft), with their grandiose cliff formations such as the "Amphitheatre" or "Cathedral Peak". Tea is cultivated in the subtropical climate of Tzaneen at the foot of the range.

The Drakensberg Mountains

Stretching over 1,000 km (620 miles) the Drakensberg Mountain Range marks the transition from the South African inner highlands to the eastern seaboard. Its northern portion, the Transvaal-Drakensberg, is under environmental protection and is designated the Blyde River Canyon Nature Reserve; the southern portion is called the Natal-Drakensberg and boasts peaks as high as 3,377 m (11,079 ft), imposing rocky giants, and secluded lakes, which since 2000 have been recognized as UNESCO World Heritages sites. Drakensberg Park has been transformed into a national park and bears the name uKhahlamba. But the region's most precious ancient sites by far are the rock paintings of the bushmen (San). More than 35,000 portrayals of wild game, hunting scenes and depictions of shaman trance ceremonies have been discovered.

A strange, almost forbidding, archaic world confronts the visitor to the mountainous Kingdom of Lesotho. Basotho ponies and mules comprise the primary means of travel and transport; at higher elevations giant agaves are prominent in the otherwise sparse vegetation.

Lesotho

The Kingdom of Lesotho, covering an area of around 30,000 sq km (18,642 sq miles), is located on the southern edge of the Drakensberg Mountains and is politically autonomous.The original inhabitants of Lesotho were the San; their rock paintings are found in numerous caves here. The Sotho moved to this region in the early 19th century. Numerous rivers, among them the Orange and the Sinque, stream through valleys at elevations of between 1,000 to 2,000 m (3,181 to 6,562 ft), often in deep ravines, bringing with them the gift of abundant greenery; in the higher reaches, the seasoned bush grass and thorny thistles weather the rough climate. The 2.2 million Sotho are mainly farmers and cattlemen. Many live in villages made up of simple rounded huts, although the city lights draw increasing numbers to the capital, Maseru.

Cecil Rhodes visited his diamond mines in a Pullman Special. Today, the "Big Hole" of Kimberley is empty. Other mines like Finsch (large picture), where diamond mining and cutting are the order of the day, make a considerable contribution to the South African economy.

Kimberley, Finsch

The diamonds at Kimberley do not lie above ground in river beds as they do in other regions but are locked into petrified volcanic chimney stone, in blue-tinged kimberlite rock. The first discoveries were made in 1869 and Kimberley soon became a city of some 10,000 inhabitants. The English adventurer and subsequently the founder of Rhodesia, Cecil Rhodes, established the De Beers Mining Company in 1880, named after a family whose claims he had bought up. Eight years later he had also absorbed his closest competitor, Barnato, and then went on to establish the De Beers Consolidated Mines, which has remained a quasi-monopoly in southern Africa until today. Finsch, one of the most modern diamond mining operations in the world, also belongs to this conglomerate. The "Big Hole", where it all began, was shut down in 1914.

In the arid northwest of the country the Orange River plunges over granite cliffs; the resulting noise, known as "augrabies" in the language of the Nama, has given the falls their name. The wandering dunes at Griquatown are also noisy.

Augrabies Falls National Park

The national park, founded in 1967, includes, in addition to the Augrabies Falls, an area of some 900 sq km (560 sq miles) of extremely arid landscape, in which the vegetation consists chiefly of quiver trees, thorn bushes and opuntia, a type of prickly pear cactus. Despite the waterless environment a rich variety of bird life has settled in the woods that follow the course of the Orange River; it is also home to desert-adapted gazelles, baboons, porcupines and black rhinos. Yet the main attraction remains the waterfalls along the Orange River, which tumble down from a point measuring between 56 and 150 m (61 and 164 yds) in width. A further natural phenomenon can be observed in the area near Griquatown: when the wind makes its way between the sand dunes it produces a powerful and uncanny sound.

The Cederberg Mountains, with their fantastic eroded rocks, characterize the southwestern region of the country. There are also many sites with cave paintings. Namaqualand, which lies to the north, is transformed into a veritable sea of flowers when spring arrives.

Namaqualand

With peaks reaching 2,027 m (6,651 ft) high, the Cederberg Mountains in the southwest are a prominent landmark. The oxide contained in the cliffs gives them a reddish hue; they have been eroded into fascinating, imaginative shapes, forming bold, soaring arches or collections of what look like toadstools sprouting from the ground. Among the best examples are the "Wolfsburg Arch" and the "Maltese Cross". In earlier times forests of Podocarpus trees dotted the landscape. These have fallen victim to tree felling and today are found only in isolated valleys. Bushmen left their paintings and engravings in caves and beneath large outcrops of rock. Along with the Nama, they were the first inhabitants of the Namaqualand, a bone-dry stretch of earth, yet one that can be transformed into a carpet of flowers by a welcome rainfall.

Lagoons with an abundance of bird life, such as the Langebaan, dot the coast northwest of Cape Town. Cape Columbine, with its white lighthouse, and the beach of the fishing village Paternoster are the most popular spots for weekend excursions by Cape Town residents.

West Coast

The coastline running from Cape Town to the northwest is an arid stretch of land, one watered only by what moisture the fog carries in; yet it is home to a wealth of plant life known as the "fynbos" – Afrikaans for "fine bush". Over 850 different varieties of plant life have been documented, among them several endemic protea. No less spectacular is the abundance of bird life, examples of which include the great cormorant or sea raven, gulls and flamingos; penguins come here to breed, and in the summer they are joined by tens of thousands of migratory birds. Fishermen all down the long stretch of the bay of Paternoster deliver another – more appetizing – prize: they pull delicious spiny lobsters out of the cold Atlantic waters; thanks to the Benguela Current, which flows northwards along the coast here, they are particularly rich in nutrients.

The key landmark of Cape Town and the entire Cape peninsula is the 1,087-m (3,566-ft) high Table Mountain, whose prominent plateau disappears beneath a white "table-cloth" when the southwest wind or "Cape Doctor" blows.

Table Mountain, The Twelve Apostles

The Khoikhoi, or Nama, called Table Mountain "hoeri kwaggo", that is "Sea Mountain". Its present name was bestowed by the first European who scaled the rise, the Portuguese Antonio da Saldanha, who baptized it "Taboa do Cabo" – "Table of the Cape"– in the year 1503. Today, no one is obliged to actually climb Table Mountain: a comfortable rotating gondola is on hand to whisk the visitor from the cable station below into the lofty heights. A number of prominent hills ring Table Mountain and Cape Town; among the best known are Lion's Head and Signal Hill in the northwest and "The Twelve Apostles" in the southwest. The deep blue waters of False Bay and the rocky outcrops that stretch far out into the sea make the panorama of Cape Town, a city of some one million inhabitants, nothing less than breathtaking.

The shimmering silhouette of Sea Point just below the Lion's Head is one of the most charming views in all of Cape Town. A lively port with a carnival atmosphere, its old colonial architecture attracts many visitors.

Cape Town

Framed by Table Mountain and other heights, embraced by the sea, rich in history – as testified by the colonial buildings up and down Long Street – and multi-cultural to boot, as is only proper for a city which has been host to so many different peoples, Cape Town is also surely one of the most beautiful cities in the world. Since its foundation by Jan van Riebeeck in 1652 the city has continued to grow. The Castle of Good Hope, erected in 1679, reflects the colonial period in both Victorian and Dutch Cape architecture; although in former times the castle bore a more ominous designation: "Donker Gat", or dark hole. In one-time suburbs such as Bo Kaap, once a settlement of Moslem Malays, traces of the Orient still linger. The main attraction for Cape Town residents, day and night, is surely the Victoria & Alfred Waterfront with its pubs, restaurants and discos.

These bright bathing huts dot the Bay of Muizenberg, one of the most popular beaches among Cape Town residents. Here at weekends no one ever seems to sleep. But even in summer the waters of the Atlantic can be invigorating, not to say downright cold.

LIFE ON THE BEACH ROUND ABOUT CAPE TOWN

Cape Town water-lovers often find themselves in a quandary when it comes to deciding between the beaches on the Atlantic side of the peninsula and those along False Bay, which also shares the waters of the Atlantic but is not affected by the cold Benguela Current. The current, which originates in the Antarctic, cools the waters along South Africa's west coast down to a tingling 12°C (54°F), while in False Bay on summer days the sea can warm up to a cosy, lukewarm 20°C (68°F). The water temperature is thus not the major attraction. Surfers and windsurfers are actually after the thrill of the mighty waves that occur between Noordhoek and Long Beach. Those who are less daredevilish are advised to choose a more congenial stretch of sand along False Bay such as the traditional seaside resort of Muizenberg, where in the 19th century the prudish Victorians also enjoyed a dip. For the sake of modesty, wooden bathing huts were erected. These still frame the beach today. More peaceful spots include the smaller bays around Simon's Town, where "The Boulders" – huge chunks of broken cliff – dot the waterline. It is not just the bathers who prefer the warmer waters of False Bay: in October and November gigantic whales, along with their young, also come to join in the fun.

In good weather, the waters of the Cape of Good Hope are a deep turquoise; an old lighthouse tops its extremity, Cape Point. For seafarers this coast was considered one of the most treacherous but also one of the most beautiful places on earth.

The Cape of Good Hope

The Portuguese sailor Bartolomeo Diaz was the first European to successfully circumnavigate the Cape in 1488, or at least the first of whom the world learned. He named it the "Cape of Storms", but it is as the Cape of Good Hope that we know it today, the name given it by the Portuguese king John II as it opened up the sea route to the Orient. The Portuguese were not the first explorers here: classical sources mention a Cape circumnavigation by the Carthaginian Hanno the Navigator, who lived around 450 BC and explored much of the African coast (although modern scholars believe that he may have reached the coast of today's Senegal). In the wake of Diaz came Portuguese seafarer and explorer Vasco da Gama and others. Da Gama's fellow countryman, Antonio do Saldanha, was the first to drop anchor in False Bay in 1503.

The view from Chapman's Peak down to Hout Bay and the road boldly hewn into the rock are among the high points of a trip around the Cape Peninsula; at the end of the journey you'll find African penguins on "Boulders" Beach.

The Cape Peninsula

The Cape Peninsula has been a nature reserve since 1998, and in 2004 it attained the status accorded to few places: recognition as a UNESCO World Nature Heritage Site. Numerous protea – robust green shrubs – spring up along the roadside, nosy baboons and shy young mountain goats, warthogs, ostriches and mountain zebras can be seen, either from the car or as you walk along the well-marked hiking paths. Other highpoints in terms of the wildlife that can be seen here are whales and dolphins. Depending on the season, both can be observed moving in groups as they make their way to False Bay. An adrenalin-pumping test of driving prowess can be undertaken on the stretch to Chapman's Peak, with unique panoramas the reward. Parking bays offer fabulous views over Hout Bay, whose selection of exquisite fish restaurants will soothe the stomach.

South Africa's vineyards have a long tradition; the first vines were planted as early as the 17th century. Today, wine producers such as Boschendal (below) earn worldwide recognition. Many wineries offer both tastings and accommodation.

WINE FROM SOUTH AFRICA

Jan van Riebeeck insisted on having vines in his settlement on the Cape, and 1654 saw the first fruits of the venture, muscatel. Soon wine from South African vineyards was being tasted and savoured in Europe's royal courts. Yet the great break through for South African wine came in the early 1990s, when the trade embargo was finally lifted. The South African winegrowers, along with their new-found European partners, started a "wine revolution", and the winegrowing regions of the western Cape – almost part of Europe – also became a popular tourist destination. Suddenly, wines were being delivered worldwide from the southern tip of Africa. At about the same time, South African winegrowers, often in cooperation with the renowned houses of Europe, began to produce first-class wines. The idyllic winegrowing areas northeast of Cape Town, which, incidentally, are also quite reminiscent of European vineyards, have also become a tourist attraction. In Paarl, for instance, there is the former Wine Growers' Cooperative, Kooperatiewe Wijnbouwers Vereeniging (page 128, second picture from top), whose KWV label adorns the bottles of many top-quality wines. Groot Constantia (above middle), the oldest wine producer in south Africa, dating back to 1685.

Cape Algulhas is Africa's southernmost point and the spot where the Atlantic and Indian Oceans meet; the lighthouse was first erected in 1848. Only a few fishing villages are to be found along this stormy coast.

Cape Agulhas

"Cape of Nails" is how the Portuguese referred to the southernmost point of the African continent, probably because of the sharp rocky outcrops that ridge the Cape, giving the storm-tossed coast a somewhat rugged appearance. Both climate and landscape are so inhospitable that you could easily imagine that the cold barren wastes of the Antarctic lie just over the horizon. A few fishing villages are scattered along the coast, separated by lonely stretches of white sandy beach. Hotagterklip is almost an artist's hideaway with its restored, thatched cottages – which have been declared historic monuments. Arniston was named after a transport ship that ran aground here in the 19th century, but takes its official name, Waenhuiskrans, from a vast cave nearby. Along with pelicans and numerous water birds, whales can also be spotted occasionally.

Isolated peaks and rock cones in the Valley of Desolation (above middle), formed by erosion at Beaufort West (above left), vast stretches covered with thornbush and green valleys with an abundance of water – these are the features of the landscapes of the Great Karoo, home to a small indigenous antelope,the cliffspringer.

Karoo, Swartberg Mountains

A semi-arid landscape with several steep elevations up to 2,000 m (6,562 ft), and around 500,000 sq km (310,700 sq miles) in area, the Karoo accounts for approximately one third of the entire land mass of South Africa. It begins just north of the Garden Route and ends between Namibia and Botswana in the Kalahari. Its transformation following the months of rainfall in February and March is nothing short of miraculous. The seeds of daisies and morning stars buried in the earth find themselves suddenly reborn, opening up and covering the Karoo with a glorious carpet. Areas of the Karoo are under environmental protection, including the Karoo National Park near Beaufort West and the Karoo Nature Reserve at Graaf-Reinet. Other regions are set aside for agricultural purposes, including the fertile valleys of the Swartberg Mountains.

The dry regions of South Africa are ideally suited to the breeding of ostriches. The farmers need to take care when handling the ostrich – these birds will not hesitate to use their beaks, or strong legs and clawed feet if provoked.

ON AN OSTRICH FARM

Farmers are increasingly changing over from the demanding requirements of cattle rearing to the relatively simple task of breeding ostriches. In South Africa, the number of ostriches is estimated at some quarter of a million; the "capital" of ostrich breeding is Oudtshoorn. Ostrich meat is now a culinary treat much in demand and products made from ostrich are on sale in many shops, from shoes and purses of ostrich leather, to eggs decorated with motifs inspired by the bush, and feather dusters and elegant feather boas. In native African mythology the ostrich has acquired the role of a somewhat conceited, but rather stupid creature. The San know how to imitate the calls of a young bird quite convincingly and are therefore able to lure the mother ostrich from her nest. While the hen is gone, the San plunder her nest; among the San such birds are both a welcome and savoured dish and provide a much-needed source of nutrition in their otherwise protein-deficient diet. The ostrich is far from tame: speed and a "brawler's nature" are its chief characteristics, so extreme caution is advised when approaching. It is worth bearing in mind that these birds may reach a height of 3 m (10 ft) and, when sprinting, can exceed 70 km/h (43 miles/h), while a single blow from their razor-sharp talons can kill a grown man.

The Garden Route leads to scenic highlights such as the Knysna Lagoon and Plettenberg Bay. Tropical forests, splendid beaches, romantic, rocky cliffs and national parks abundant in wildlife abound.

The Garden Route

South Africa's most famous landscape is the Garden Route; it runs some 200 km (124 miles) between Mossel Bay and Storm River along the Indian Ocean, rich in bays and inlets. Among the best known sights is Knysna Lagoon; from the rocky heights of Knysna Head the view is nothing less than fantastic. Knysna Forest, in the backlands of South Africa, is a large subtropical forest and home to a good number of 800-year-old Padocarpus trees; the forest elephant, all but decimated, is attempting a comeback here. Plettenberg Bay is certainly the best location for swimmers; holiday hotels and elegant beach villas pepper the sandy-white shores. When winter comes to the south, whales come to the bay to bear their young. In the Tsitsikamma National Park an impressive stretch of ancient forest has been designated a nature reserve.

Blessed with a tenth of all flowering plant forms in existence, South Africa has many more species than Europe. It is difficult to ignore the giant *Protea cynaroides*, a tough lustrous bloom, the national flower of the Republic of South Africa.

THE FLORA OF THE CAPE PROVINCE

Relative to its area, the Cape Province has the greatest abundance of flora on earth – richer by far than any tropical rainforests: here some 6,000 flowering plants are to be found, approximately 32 per cent of which are endemic to the region. Protea and heather bells are particularly well represented, with around 450 variations. In 2004, the flora of the Cape Province achieved recognition as a UNESCO World Nature Heritage. Eight regions have since been declared nature reserves. Although this entire area, itself encompassing barely 533 sq km (331 sq miles), is only one half of a per cent of the entire continent of Africa, it is, nevertheless, home and haven to some 20 per cent of all flowering plants. The plants here have become accustomed to the seasonal bushfires, which come and go. For example, the fynbos is a deciduous hardwood, and is unique as bushfires leave it unscathed. The diversity of the plant life in Cape Province is quite exceptional, making it a haven for nature lovers and ramblers alike. Plants proliferate at speed, pollinated with the aid of the wind, or by insects attracted by the flowers' petals and strong scent. During August and September, whole areas of the Cape Province are carpeted with a mass of beautiful wild flowers.

South Africa is an absolute “must” for every railway buff. Drawn by the steam-powered Outeniqua Choo-Tjoe you can simply sit back as the trusty old “iron horse” chugs along the Garden Route. The Blue Train (small picture) is the connection between Cape Town and Johannesburg.

THE "BLUE TRAIN" AND THE "OUTENIQUA CHOO-TJOE"

From the Cape to Cairo – by train! This was Cecil Rhodes' vision – yet it remained a dream. However, South Africa nevertheless succeeded in establishing numerous railway connections. It can justifiably be proud of its over 36,000 km (22,370 miles) of rail network transporting both passengers and freight. Old steam-powered trains are also still in service, crossing over landscapes of extraordinary beauty, especially in the Cape Province. The most famous and expensive means of rail travel is without a doubt the Rovos Rail running from the Cape to Kruger National Park or, on occasion, further. The compartments have been restored to their original glory, and in such surroundings the great days of rail travel come alive again. No less luxurious, evoking a bygone age of grace and elegance, is the Blue Train which travels between Cape Town and Johannesburg, and in high season continues on to Port Elizabeth. Passengers on the Blue Train expect, and receive, only the best in service, cuisine and comfort. A pleasant day trip from George to Knysna and back can be taken on the Outeniqua Choo Tjoe, the last remaining continually operated passenger steam train in Africa. Yet a trip by train in South Africa can be risky – timetables are not always kept to and the safety of passengers is not always assured.

Tsitsikama National Park on the Garden Route brings together very disparate landscapes: the arid, rocky coastland, the dunes of Nature's Valley as well as regions with thick forest undergrowth. The sea is also under environmental protection.

Tsitsikama National Park

"Clear Water" – "Tsitsikama" – was the name given by the Khoikhoi to this stretch of coast, which extends some 80 km (50 miles) eastwards from Plettenberg Bay. Since 1964 the inaccessible coast and the underwater world found between the sandy inlets of Nature's Bay and the mouth of Storms River have been protected. There are two quite distinct forms of vegetation found here: the fynbos, with its distinctive protea, near the coast, and the virgin forests of Podcarpus trees found in some valleys. One experience not to miss is a tour of the forest canopy – a kind of aerial trek with a bird's eye view along walkways erected high up among the treetops. The marine reserve extends 5 km (3.1 miles) from the coast and protects numerous species of marine plant and animal life, among them 65 types of fish and dolphins and whales.

In 1931, the year in which the Addo Elephant Park was first established, just 11 cape elephants were living here. Today, fortunately, their number has increased to some 300 creatures. The female of the species is easily recognized: they lack the tusks of the males.

Addo Elephant Park

Addo Elephant National Park is renowned for its Cape elephants. Experts attribute the lack of tusks in the females to inbreeding among the relatively small and isolated herd groupings. Alongside elephants, Cape buffalo, the "black rhino", antelopes, brown-white kudus and the duiker, a smallish breed of antelope, can be observed when they come to drink. The Zuur Range, with its unique leopard population, has been placed under environmental protection since 1995. Should ambitious planning be realized, the second largest national park in southern Africa will be established here, with the "Big Five" (lion, elephant, buffalo, leopard and rhino) of African wildlife present and correct, and ready for the camera lens. A large area for protected marine life, including the island group of St Croix and the Bird Islands – not excluding Addo – will also be included.

A variety of different landscapes, animals and cultures await the visitor to southern Africa. And it is precisely thanks to this variety that what was once known as the "Dark Continent" enjoys such popularity today. Stellenbosch is the second oldest European settlement on the Cape; it lies in a fertile fruit and winegrowing region (large picture: Restaurant Lord Neethling on the Neethlingshof Estate).

ATLAS

Namibia comprises three main regions. The Namibian Desert is bordered by the coast to the west and the Great Escarpment to the east, while beyond that lies the land-locked basin of the Kalahari and the large salt water depression, the Etosha Pan. Botswana is for the most part a broad highland between the Zambezi River in the north and the Limpopo and Molopo Rivers in the south. Inland from South Africa's coastal region lie the interior plateau and the Great Escarpment, dominated by the Drakensberg Mountains.

It is believed that the Herero moved from the eastern African savannah to southwestern Africa during the early 16th century. A semi-nomadic people, they lived from cattle rearing and were in search of new pastureland.

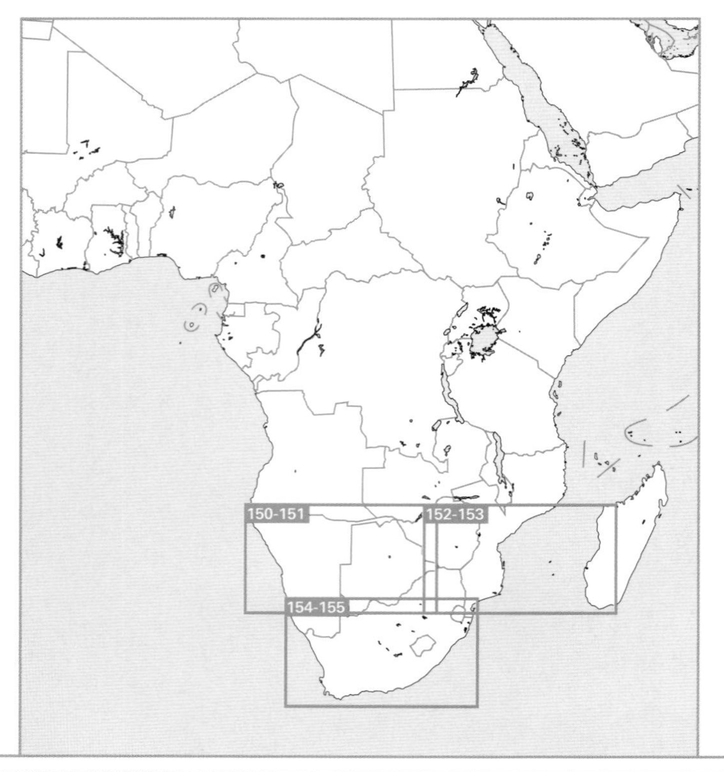

MAP KEY
1 : 4500,000

- Motorway
- Dual carriageway
- Trunk road
- Important main road
- Main road
- Secondary road
- Track
- Railway
- Ferry
- International boundary
- Administrative boundary
- National and nature park boundary
- Reservation
- Important airport
- Airport

KEY

The maps on the following pages show southern Africa on a scale of 1:450,000. Geographical details have been supplemented by numerous items of useful information: the traffic and transport system has been mapped out in great detail and symbols indicate all the important sights and tourist destinations by location and type. The names of cities that tourists may find particularly interesting are highlighted in yellow. UNESCO World Natural Heritage Sites are specially marked for convenience.

SYMBOLS

- Motorway
- Railway line
- Shipping route
- UNESCO World Heritage (Natural)
- Mountain landscape
- Rock landscape
- Ravine/canyon
- Extinct volcano
- Cave
- River landscape
- Waterfall/rapids
- Lake country
- Desert
- Fossil site
- Nature park
- National Park (landscape)
- National Park (flora)
- National Park (fauna)
- National Park (culture)
- Biosphere reserve
- Wildlife reserve
- Whale watching
- Turtle conservation area
- Protected area for sea lions/seals
- Protected area for Penguins
- Zoo/safari park
- Crocodile farm
- Coastal landscape
- Beach
- Coral reef
- Underwater reserve
- UNESCO World Heritage (Cultural)
- Remarkable City
- Pre- and early history
- Prehistoric rockscape

- Early African cultures
- Places of Christian cultural interest
- Places of Islamic cultural interest
- Places of Hindu cultural interest
- Pl. of other religions cultural interest
- Cultural landscape
- Historic cityscape
- Remarkable skyline
- Castle/fortress/fort
- Technical/industrial monument
- Dam
- Lighthouse worth seeing
- Remarkable bridge
- Tomb/grave
- Theater of war/battlefield
- Monument
- Memorial
- Space telescope
- Market
- Festivals
- Museum
- Theater
- Arena/stadium
- Racetrack
- Golf
- Horse racing
- Skiing
- Sailing
- Diving
- Wind surfing
- Surfing
- Canoeing/rafting
- Sea port
- Deep-sea fishing
- Beach resort
- Mineral spring/thermal spa
- Amusement park
- Casino
- Hill resort
- Lodge

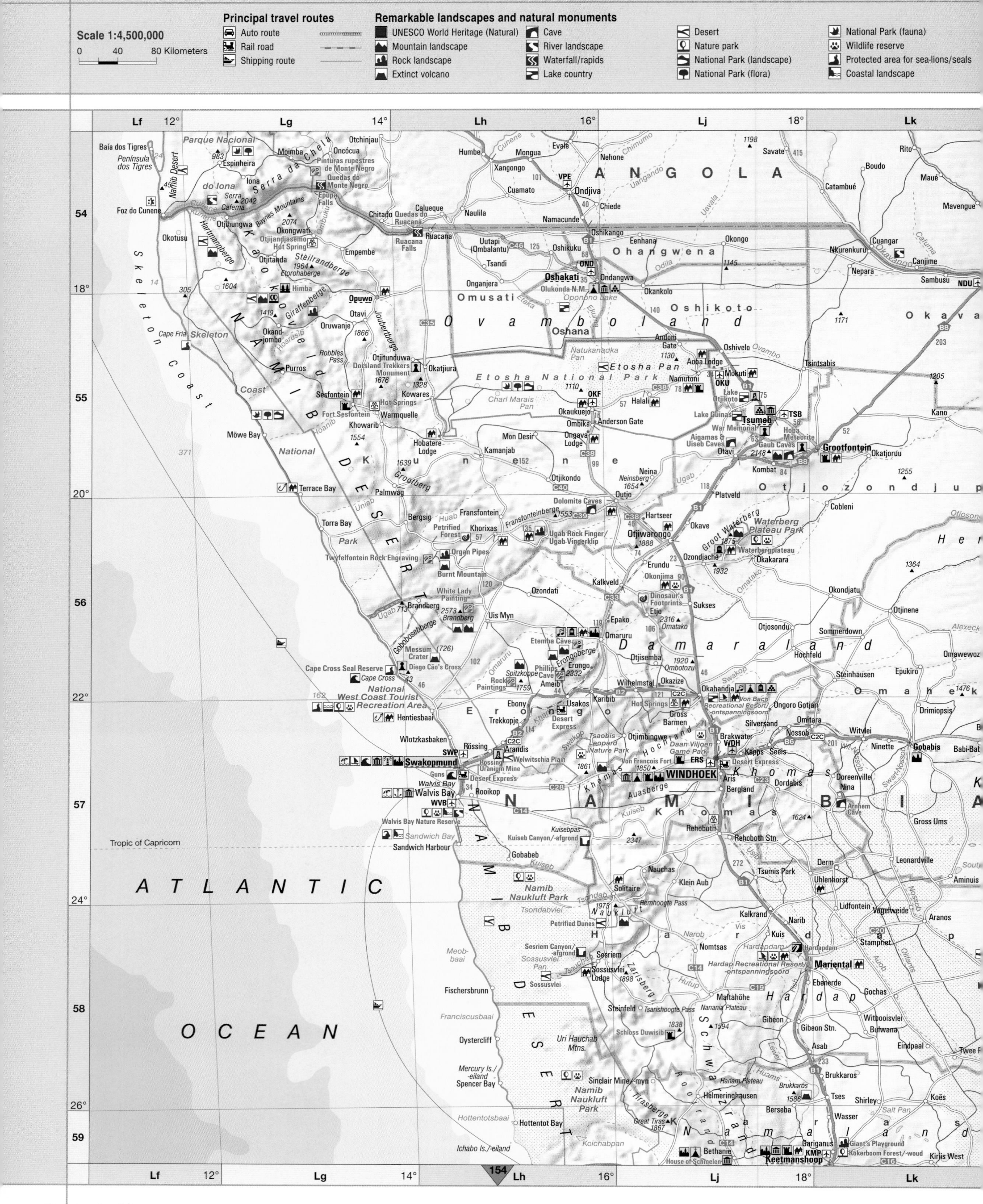

Scale 1:4,500,000
0 40 80 Kilometers
Principal travel routes
Auto route
Rail road
Shipping route
Remarkable landscapes and natural monuments
UNESCO World Heritage (Natural)
Mountain landscape
Rock landscape
Extinct volcano
Cave
River landscape
Waterfall/rapids
Lake country
Desert
Nature park
National Park (landscape)
National Park (flora)
National Park (fauna)
Wildlife reserve
Protected area for sea-lions/seals
Coastal landscape
Lf 12° Lg 14° Lh 16° Lj 18° Lk
54
55
56
57
58
59
18°
20°
22°
24°
26°
A N G O L A
Ondjiva
Oshakati
Ovamboland
Omusati
Oshana
Ohangwena
Oshikoto
Okavango
Otjozondjupa
Etosha National Park
Etosha Pan
Skeleton Coast
Skeleton Coast National Park
Kaokoveld
NAMIB DESERT
Opuwo
Tsumeb
Grootfontein
Otjiwarongo
Outjo
Waterberg Plateau Park
Damaraland
Erongo
Brandberg
Twyfelfontein Rock Engraving
Cape Cross Seal Reserve
National West Coast Tourist Recreation Area
Hentiesbaai
Swakopmund
Walvis Bay
Walvis Bay Nature Reserve
Sandwich Harbour
Okahandja
WINDHOEK
Khomas
Khomas Hochland
Rehoboth
Gobabis
NAMIBIA
Namib Naukluft Park
Sesriem
Sossusvlei
Mariental
Hardap
Keetmanshoop
Lüderitz
Hottentot Bay
Spencer Bay
Great Karas
Namaland
Tropic of Capricorn
ATLANTIC OCEAN
Lf 12° Lg 14° 154 Lh 16° Lj 18° Lk

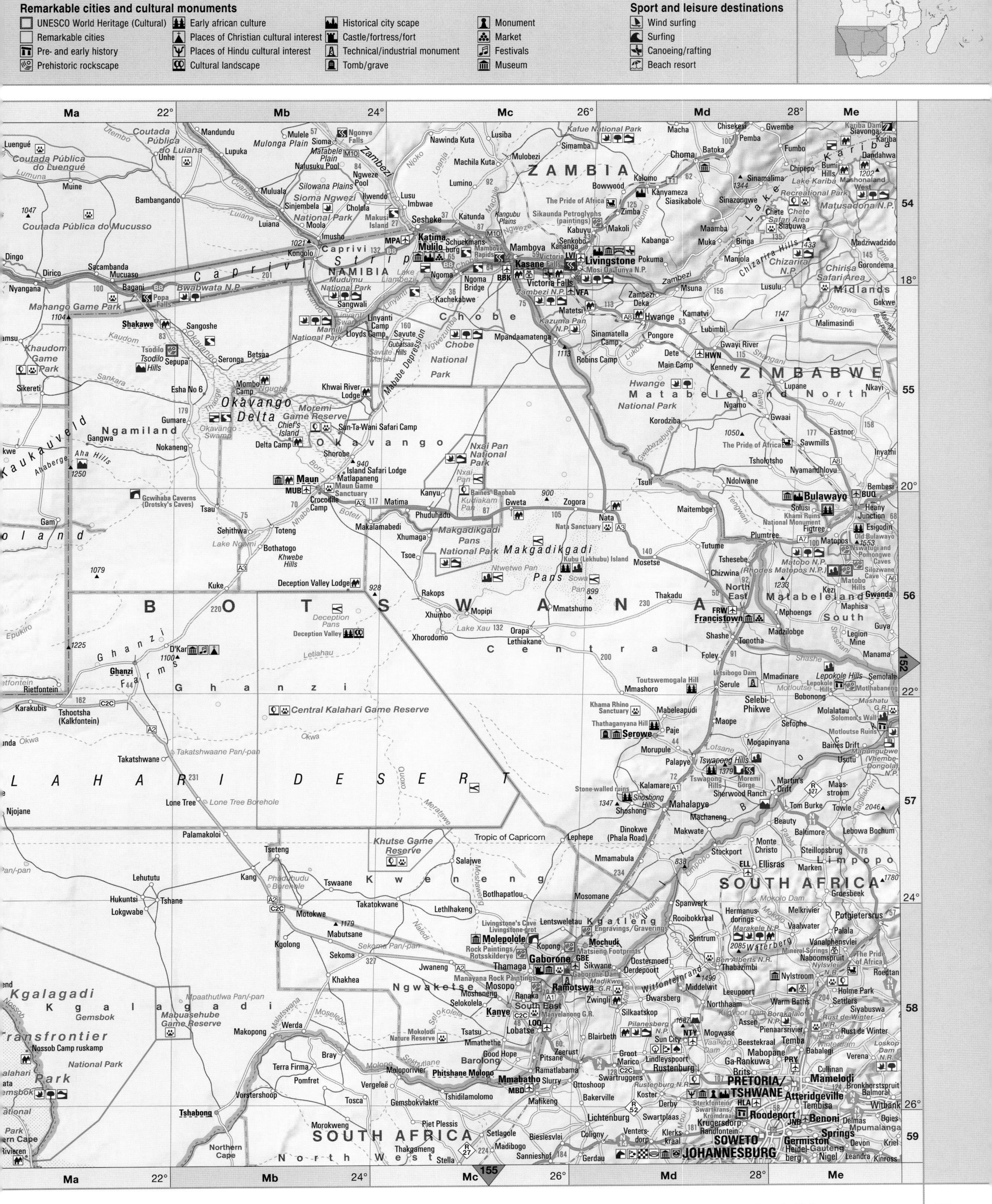

Remarkable cities and cultural monuments
UNESCO World Heritage (Cultural)
Remarkable cities
Pre- and early history
Prehistoric rockscape
Early african culture
Places of Christian cultural interest
Places of Hindu cultural interest
Cultural landscape
Historical city scape
Castle/fortress/fort
Technical/industrial monument
Tomb/grave
Monument
Market
Festivals
Museum
Sport and leisure destinations
Wind surfing
Surfing
Canoeing/rafting
Beach resort
Ma
22°
Mb
24°
Mc
26°
Md
28°
Me
54
55
56
57
58
59
18°
20°
22°
24°
26°
ZAMBIA
ZIMBABWE
NAMIBIA
BOTSWANA
SOUTH AFRICA
Caprivi Strip
Okavango Delta
Ngamiland
Makgadikgadi Pans
KALAHARI DESERT
Ghanzi Farms
Central Kalahari Game Reserve
Chobe National Park
Hwange National Park
Kgalagadi Transfrontier Park
Tropic of Capricorn
Lake Kariba
Livingstone
Victoria Falls
Kasane
Katima Mulilo
Maun
Francistown
Bulawayo
Serowe
Mahalapye
Molepolole
Gaborone
Ramotswa
Kanye
Lobatse
Mafikeng
Mmabatho
Rustenburg
PRETORIA/TSHWANE
JOHANNESBURG
SOWETO
Roodepoort
Germiston
Benoni
Springs
Mamelodi
Ghanzi
Tshabong
Hwange
Selebi-Phikwe
Palapye
Nata
Gweta
Orapa
Kang
Lephepe
Sesheke
Mambova
Zambezi
Limpopo
152
155

Scale 1:4,500,000
0 40 80 Kilometers
Principal travel routes
Auto route
Rail road
Shipping route
Remarkable landscapes and natural monuments
UNESCO World Heritage (Natural)
Mountain landscape
Rock landscape
Ravine/canyon
Cave
River landscape
Waterfall/rapids
Lake country
Fossil site
Nature park
National Park (landscape)
National Park (flora)
National Park (fauna)
Wildlife reserve
Whale watching
Turtle conservation area
Md 28° Me 30° Mf 32° Mg 34° Mh 36°
ZIMBABWE
MOZAMBIQUE
SOUTH AFRICA
BOTSWANA
HARARE
MAPUTO
PRETORIA/TSHWANE
Bulawayo
Gweru
Mutare
Chimoio
Beira
Masvingo
Chitungwiza
Kwekwe
Kadoma
Marondera
Messina
Pietersburg/Polokwane
Nelspruit
Mbabane
Inhambane
Maxixe
Xai-Xai
Lake Kariba
Mashonaland
Midlands
Manicaland
Masvingo
Matabeleland North
Matabeleland South
Limpopo
Mpumalanga
Great Limpopo Transfrontier Park
Parque Nacional de Gorongoza
Parque Nacional de Banhine
Parque Nacional de Zinave
Kruger National Park
Baía de Maputo
Me 30° Mf 32° 155 Mg 34° Mh 36° Mj

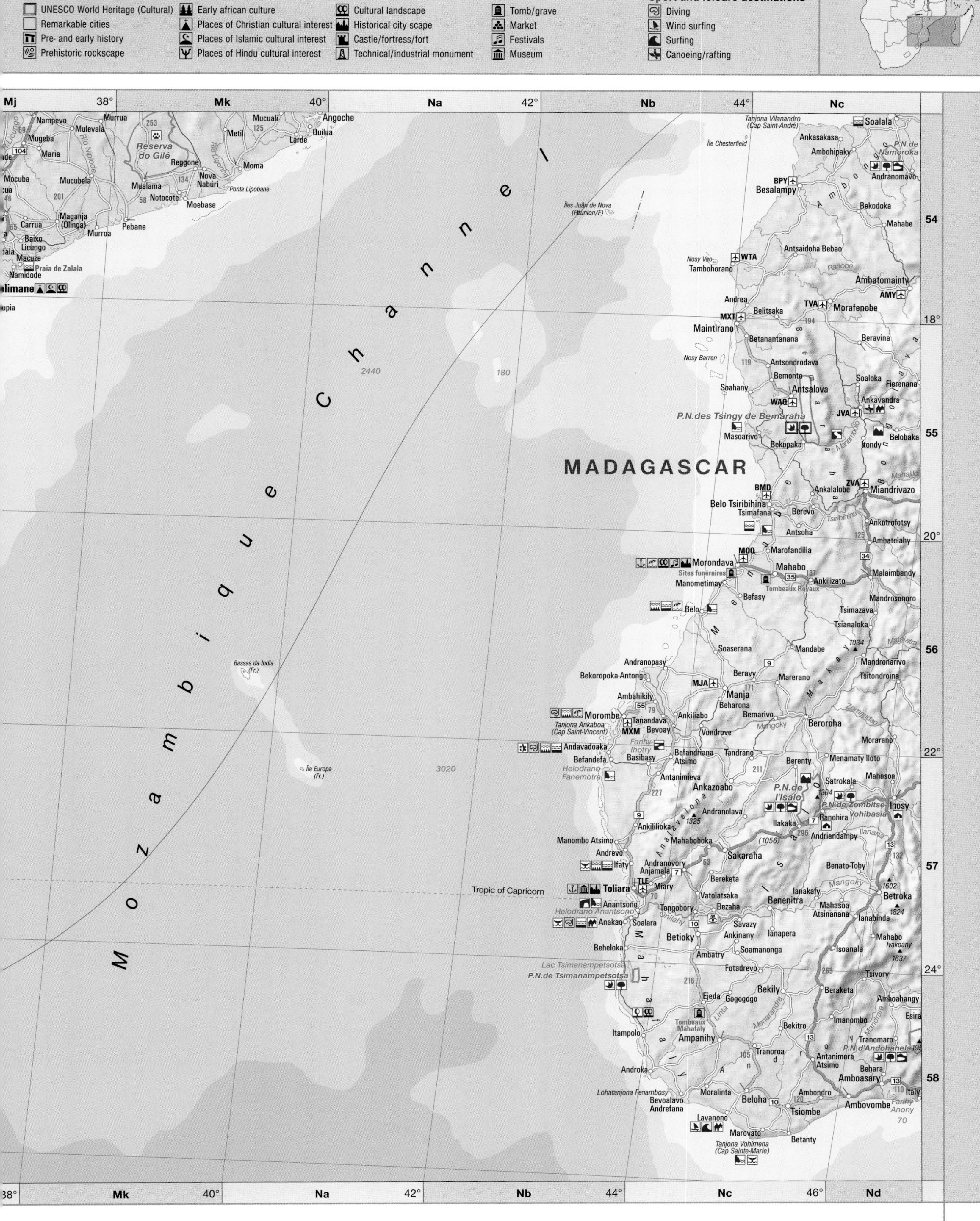
Remarkable cities and cultural monuments
UNESCO World Heritage (Cultural)
Remarkable cities
Pre- and early history
Prehistoric rockscape
Early african culture
Places of Christian cultural interest
Places of Islamic cultural interest
Places of Hindu cultural interest
Cultural landscape
Historical city scape
Castle/fortress/fort
Technical/industrial monument
Tomb/grave
Market
Festivals
Museum
Sport and leisure destinations
Diving
Wind surfing
Surfing
Canoeing/rafting
Mj
38°
Mk
40°
Na
42°
Nb
44°
Nc
46°
Nd
54
55
56
57
58
18°
20°
22°
24°
Mozambique Channel
MADAGASCAR
Nampevo
Murrua
Mulevala
Mugeba
Maria
Reserva do Gilé
Mucuali
Metil
Angoche
Quilua
Larde
Moma
Reggone
Mocuba
Mucubela
Mualama
Nova Nabúri
Ponta Lipobane
Notocote
Moebase
Maganja (Olinga)
Carrua
Murroa
Pebane
Baixo Licungo
Macuze
Praia de Zalala
Namidode
Quelimane
Île Chesterfield
Tanjona Vilanandro (Cap Saint-André)
Soalala
Ankasakasa
Ambohipaky
P.N.de Namoroka
Andranomavo
Besalampy
Bekodoka
Mahabe
Îles Juan de Nova (Réunion/F)
Nosy Vao
Tambohorano
Antsaidoha Bebao
Ambatomainty
Andrea
Belitsaka
Morafenobe
Maintirano
Betanantanana
Beravina
Nosy Barren
Antsondrodava
Bemonto
Antsalova
Soahany
Soaloka
Fierenana
Ankavandra
2440
180
P.N.des Tsingy de Bemaraha
Masoarivo
Bekopaka
Belobaka
Itondy
Ankalalobe
Miandrivazo
Belo Tsiribihina
Tsimafana
Berevo
Antsoha
Ankotrofotsy
Ambatolahy
Marofandilia
Morondava
Mahabo
Sites funéraires
Manometimay
Ankilizato
Tombeaux Royaux
Malaimbandy
Befasy
Mandrosonoro
Belo
Tsimazava
Tsianaloka
Soaserana
Mandabe
Andranopasy
Bekoropoka-Antongo
Beravy
Marerano
Mandronarivo
Tsitondroina
Bassas da India (Fr.)
Ambahikily
Manja
Beharona
Bemarivo
Morombe
Tanandava
Ankiliabo
Beroroha
Tanjona Ankaboa (Cap Saint-Vincent)
MXM
Bevoay
Vondrove
Andavadoaka
Befandefa
Basibasy
Befandriana Atsimo
Tandrano
Berenty
Menamaty Iloto
Morarano
Île Europa (Fr.)
3020
Helodrano Fanemotra
Antanimieva
Ankazoabo
Satrokala
Mahasoa
P.N.de l'Isalo
P.N.de Zombitse-Vohibasia
Ihosy
Andranolava
Ilakaka
Ranohira
Ankililioka
Andriandampy
Manombo Atsimo
Mahaboboka
Andrevo
Sakaraha
Ifaty
Andranovory
Anjamala
Bereketa
Benato-Toby
Tropic of Capricorn
Toliara
Miary
Vatolatsaka
Ianakafy
Betroka
Benenitra
Anantsono
Helodrano Anantsono
Tongobory
Bezaha
Mahasoa Atsinanana
Ianabinda
Anakao
Soalara
Savazy
Betioky
Ankinany
Ianapera
Mahabo
Beheloka
Ambatry
Soamanonga
Isoanala
Lac Tsimanampetsotsa
P.N.de Tsimanampetsotsa
Fotadrevo
Tsivory
Bekily
Beraketa
Ejeda
Gogogogo
Amboahangy
Tombeaux Mahafaly
Imanombo
Esira
Itampolo
Ampanihy
Bekitro
Tranomaro
P.N.d'Andohahela
Tranoroa
Antanimora Atsimo
Androka
Behara
Amboasary
Lohatanjona Fenambosy
Moralinta
Ambondro
Bevoalavo
Andrefana
Beloha
Tsiombe
Ambovombe
Italy
Faux Cap
Lavanono
Marovato
Betanty
Tanjona Vohimena (Cap Sainte-Marie)

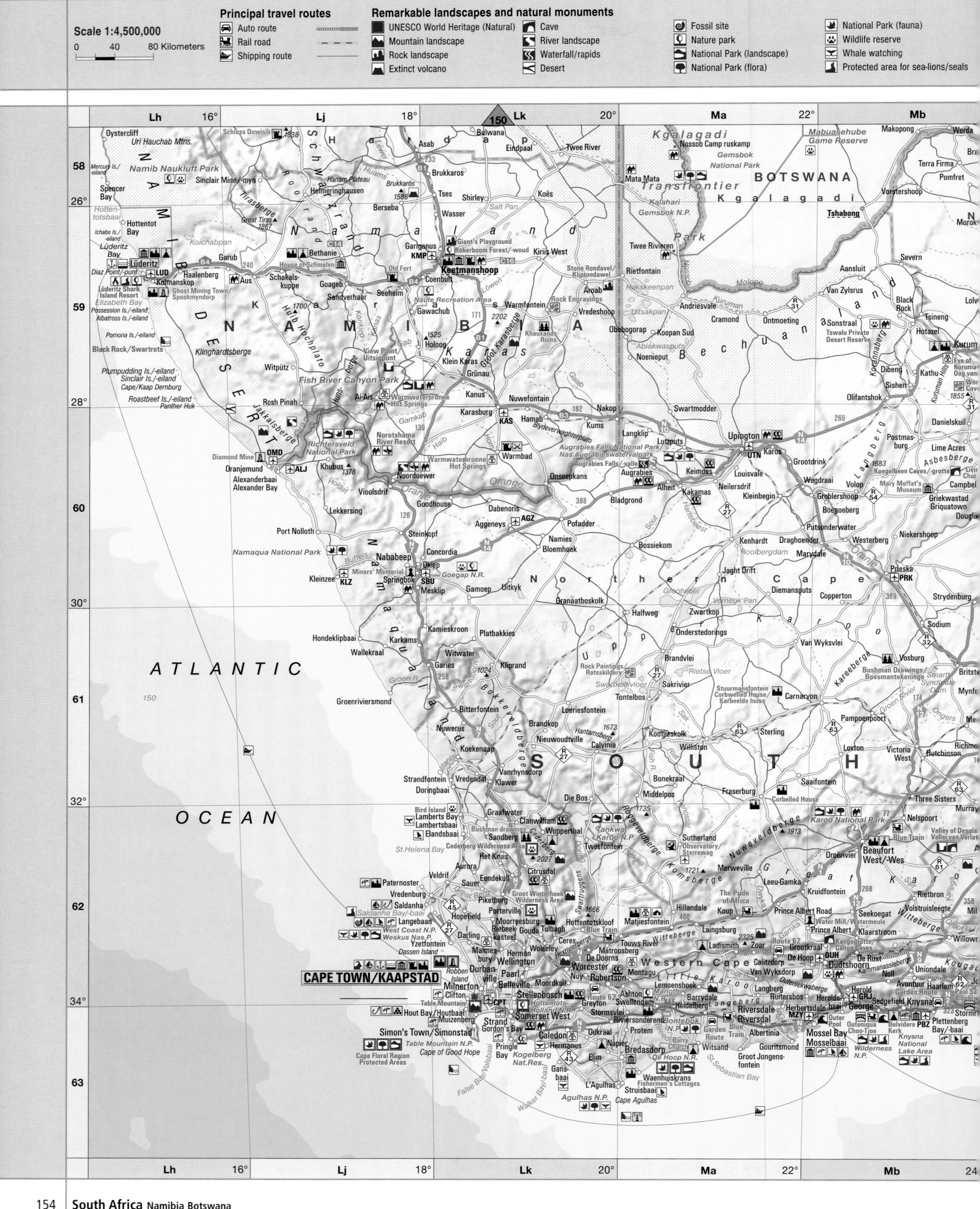

Scale 1:4,500,000
0 40 80 Kilometers
Principal travel routes
Auto route
Rail road
Shipping route
Remarkable landscapes and natural monuments
UNESCO World Heritage (Natural)
Mountain landscape
Rock landscape
Extinct volcano
Cave
River landscape
Waterfall/rapids
Desert
Fossil site
Nature park
National Park (landscape)
National Park (flora)
National Park (fauna)
Wildlife reserve
Whale watching
Protected area for sea-lions/seals
Lh
16°
Lj
18°
150
Lk
20°
Ma
22°
Mb
58
26°
59
28°
60
30°
61
32°
62
34°
63
ATLANTIC
OCEAN
NAMIBIA
BOTSWANA
SOUTH
Namib Naukluft Park
NAMIB DESERT
Namaqualand
Bushmanland
Kgalagadi Transfrontier Park
Northern Cape
Upper Karoo
Western Cape
Little Karoo
Great Karoo
Fish River Canyon Park
Richtersveld National Park
Namaqua National Park
Augrabies Falls National Park
Karoo National Park
Table Mountain N.P.
Agulhas N.P.
Oystercliff
Spencer Bay
Hottentot Bay
Lüderitz
Kolmanskop
Aus
Keetmanshoop
Bethanie
Helmeringhausen
Brukkaros
Mariental
Gariganus
Grünau
Karasburg
Rosh Pinah
Ai-Ais
Noordoewer
Oranjemund
Alexanderbaai
Port Nolloth
Springbok
Nababeep
Kleinzee
Pofadder
Upington
Kakamas
Augrabies
Keimoes
Kenhardt
Prieska
Tshabong
Twee Rivieren
Hondeklipbaai
Kamieskroon
Garies
Bitterfontein
Nuwerus
Vanrhynsdorp
Vredendal
Calvinia
Nieuwoudtville
Loeriesfontein
Brandvlei
Williston
Carnarvon
Fraserburg
Sutherland
Lambert's Bay
Clanwilliam
Citrusdal
Paternoster
Vredenburg
Saldanha
Langebaan
Darling
Malmesbury
Wellington
Paarl
Worcester
Robertson
Montagu
Ceres
Tulbagh
Laingsburg
Matjiesfontein
Beaufort West/-Wes
Prince Albert
Oudtshoorn
Calitzdorp
Ladismith
Barrydale
Swellendam
Heidelberg
Riversdale
Mosselbaai
George
Knysna
Plettenberg Bay/-baai
Uniondale
CAPE TOWN/KAAPSTAD
Robben Island
Stellenbosch
Somerset West
Hout Bay/Houtbaai
Simon's Town/Simonstad
Cape of Good Hope
Gordon's Bay
Caledon
Hermanus
Gansbaai
Bredasdorp
Struisbaai
L'Agulhas
Cape Agulhas
Waenhuiskrans
Witsand
Stilbaai
False Bay/Valsbaai
Walker Bay/-baai
St.Helena Bay
Saldanha Bay/-baai

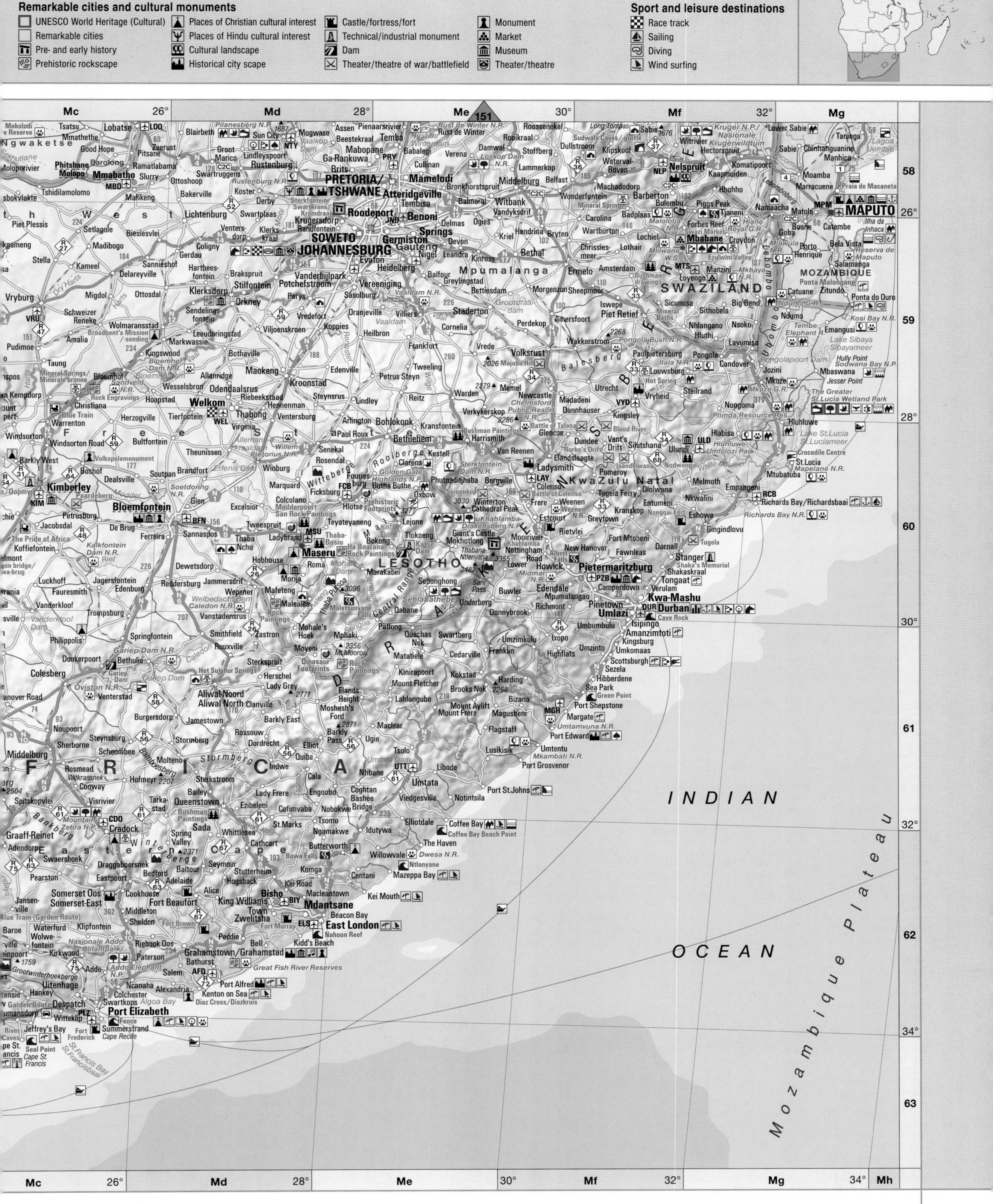

Remarkable cities and cultural monuments
UNESCO World Heritage (Cultural)
Remarkable cities
Pre- and early history
Prehistoric rockscape
Places of Christian cultural interest
Places of Hindu cultural interest
Cultural landscape
Historical city scape
Castle/fortress/fort
Technical/industrial monument
Dam
Theater/theatre of war/battlefield
Monument
Market
Museum
Theater/theatre
Sport and leisure destinations
Race track
Sailing
Diving
Wind surfing
PRETORIA/TSHWANE
SOWETO
JOHANNESBURG
MAPUTO
SWAZILAND
MOZAMBIQUE
LESOTHO
Mpumalanga
KwaZulu Natal
Maseru
Mbabane
Bloemfontein
Kimberley
Pietermaritzburg
Durban
East London
Port Elizabeth
Grahamstown/Grahamstad
Mdantsane
Umlazi
Kwa-Mashu
Welkom
Nelspruit
INDIAN
OCEAN
Mozambique Plateau

The entries in the index refer to the main text and the maps. Each index entry is followed by a symbol (explained on p.149), which indicates the type of sight referred to. The symbol is followed by a page reference to the main text. Finally, there are details of websites that will provide up-to-date information on the places of interest and the various sights described in this book. Most of the places described in the main text will also be found in the map section, which provides a wealth of further information for visitors.

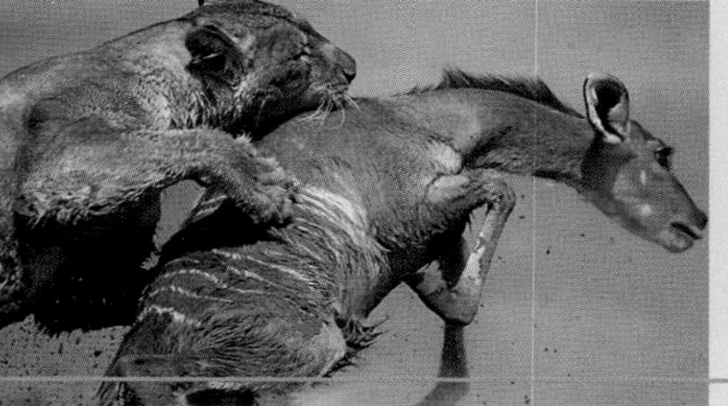

From left to right: in the Addo Elephant Park; at Cape Agulhas – the southernmost point of Africa; bathing huts on Muizenburg Bay (Cape Town); in Etosha National Park.

Place	Map page	Grid	Text page	Website
Goegap Nature Reserve	154	Lk60		www.go2africa.com
Golden Gate Highlands N.P.	155	Me60		www.parks-sa.co.za/parks/goldengate/default.html
Gordon's Bay	154	Lk63		www.southafrica-travel.net/westcape/cape_gordonsb.htm
Graaff-Reinet	155	Mc62		www.graaffreinet.co.za
Grahamstad	155	Md62		www.grahamstown.co.za
Grahamstown	155	Md62		www.grahamstown.co.za
Greater St. Lucia Wetland Park			95	
Great Fish River Reserves	155	Md62		http://home.intekom.com/african_lioness/reserves.html
Great Karoo	154	Ma62	132f.	www1.capetourism.org/regional_info.asp?Mode=E&RegID=18
Green Point	155	Mf61		www.wannasurf.com
Griekwastad	154	Mb60		www.places.co.za/html/griekwastad.html
Griquatown	154	Mb60	112f.	www.places.co.za/html/griekwastad.html
Groot Constantia			129	
Grootfontein	150	Lk55		www.namibia-travel.net/centralnamibia/grootfontein.htm
Groot Winterhoek Wilderness Area	154	Lk62		http://whc.unesco.org/pg.cfm?cid=31&id_site=1007
Gross Barmen	150	Lj57		www.namibiatourism.com
Guns	150	Lh57		www.wannasurf.com/spot/Africa/Namibia/guns/index.html
Gweta	151	Mc56		www.go2africa.com/botswana/makgadikgadi-pans/gweta
Ha Baroana Rock Paintings	155	Md60		www.seelesotho.com
Halali	150	Lj55		www.namibiatourism.com
Hans Merensky Nature Reserve	152	Mf57		www.go2africa.com
Hardapdam	150	Lj58	61	http://namibia.safari.co.za/africa_hardap.html
Hardapontspanningsoord	150	Lj58		www.namibiatourism.com
Hardap Recreational Resort	150	Lj58		www.namibiatourism.com
Hartmannberge	150	Lg54		www.namibiatourism.com
Hentiesbaai	150	Lh57		www.namibiatourism.com
Hermanus	154	Lk63		www.hermanus.co.za
Hexrivier Mountains	154	Lk62		www.capetourism.org
Hlane Royal Game Reserve	155	Mf59		www.biggameparks.org
Hluhluwe	155	Mg60		www.hluhluwe.co.za
Hluhluwe-Umfolozi Park	155	Mf60	92f.	http://zululand.kzn.org.za/zululand/about/63.html
Hoba Meteorite	150	Lj55		www.namibiatourism.com
Hobatere Lodge	150	Lh55		www.namibiatourism.com
Hohe Karoo	154	Lk61	132f.	
Hotagterklip			131	
Hot Sulphur Springs	155	Md61		www.go2africa.com/south-africa/central/aliwal-north
Hottentots-Holland Nature Reserve	154	Lk63		http://whc.unesco.org/pg.cfm?cid=31&id_site=1007
House of Schmelen	154	Lj59		www.namibian.org/travel/namibia/bethanie.html
Hout Bay	154	Lk63		www.go2africa.com/south-africa/cape-peninsula/hout-bay
Isandhlwana	155	Mf60		http://battlefields.kzn.org.za/battlefields/about/29.html 18
Itala Nature Reserve	155	Mf59		www.go2africa.com
Jeffrey's Bay	155	Mc63		www.go2africa.com/south-africa/eastern-cape/jeffreys-bay
Johannesburg	155	Md59	76f.	www.joburg.org.za
Kakamas	154	Ma60		www.go2africa.com/south-africa/augrabies/kakamas
Kalahari	151	Ma57	70f.	www.e-gnu.com
Kalahari Gemsbok N.P.	154	Ma59		www.parks-sa.co.za/parks/kgalagadi/default.html
Kalkfontein Dam Nature Reserve	155	Mc60		www.go2africa.com
Kango grotto	154	Mb62		www.cangocaves.co.za
Kaokoveld	150	Lg54	12ff.	www.namibiatourism.com
Kap Agulhas	154	Ma63	130f.	www.southafrica-travel.net/westcape/overberg_02.htm
Kap Columbine			116	
Karibib	150	Lh56	33	
Karoo			132f.	
Karoo N.P.	154	Mb62	133	www.parks-sa.co.za/parks/Karoo/default.html
Kasane	151	Mc54		www.botswana-tourism.gov.bw
Katatura			41	
Katima Mulilo	151	Mc54		www.go2africa.com/namibia/caprivi/katima-mulilo
Katse Dam	155	Me60		www.seelesotho.com/travel/info/waterproject.htm
Keetmanshoop	154	Lk59	57	www.namibiatourism.com
Keimoes	154	Ma60		www.go2africa.com/south-africa/augrabies/keimoes
Kei Mouth	155	Me62		www.southafrica-travel.net/eastcape/e_keimouth.htm
Kenton on Sea	155	Md62		www.kenton.co.za
Kgalagadi Transfrontier Park	151	Ma58		www.parks-sa.co.za/parks/kgalagadi/default.html
Khama Rhino Sanctuary	151	Md57		www.khamarhinosanctuary.org
Khaudom Game Park	151	Ma55		www.namibiatourism.com
Khauxanas Ruins	154	Lk59		www.klausdierks.com/Khauxanas
Khomas Highland	150	Lh57		http://namibia.safari.co.za/africa_windhoek.html
Khorixas	150	Lh56		www.namibiatourism.com
Khutse Game Reserve	151	Mc57		www.botswana-tourism.gov.bw
Khwai River Lodge	151	Mb55		www.botswana.co.za/khwai-river-lodge-botswana.html
Kimberley	155	Mc60	110f.	www.kimberley.co.za
Kiripoteb			42	
Klaserie Nature Reserve	152	Mf58		www.go2africa.com

Place	Map page	Grid	Text page	Website
Klasies River Caves	155	Mc63		http://whc.unesco.org
Kleine Karoo	154	Ma62	132f.	www.southafrica-travel.net/eastcape/ekaroo.htm
Klerksdorp	155	Md59		www.klerksdorp.org
Knysna	154	Mb63	137	www.visitknysna.com
Knysna National Lake Area	154	Mb63		www.parks-sa.co.za/parks/knysna/default.html
Koegelbeen Caves	154	Mb60		www.northerncape.org.za/diamondfields/placesofinterest.html
Koegelbeen grotto	154	Mb60		www.northerncape.org.za/diamondfields/placesofinterest.html
Kogelberg Nature Reserve	154	Lk63		www.capenature.org.za/Nature_Reserves/html/kogelberg.html
Kokerboom Forest	154	Lk59		www.namibiatourism.com
Kokerboomwoud	154	Lk59		www.namibiatourism.com
Kolmanskop	154	Lh59	58f.	
Kooperatiewe Wijnbouwers Vereeniging			129	
Kosi Bay Nature Reserve	155	Mg59		www.zulunet.co.za/kfl/kosi.htm
Kromdraai	155	Md59		http://whc.unesco.org/pg.cfm?cid=31&id_site=915
Kruger N.P. = Nasionale Krugerwildtuin	152	Mf57	86f.	www.krugerpark.co.za
Kubu (Lekhubu) Island	151	Mc56		www.botswana-tourism.gov.bw/tourism/attractions/kubu.html
Kuisebfagrond	150	Lh57		www.namibiatourism.com
Kuiseb Canyon	150	Lh57		www.namibiatourism.com
Kunene	150	Lg54	12f.	www.travel.za.net/cunene-river-namibia.html
Kuruman	154	Mb59		www.go2africa.com/south-africa/diamond-fields/kuruman
KwaZulu-Natal	155	Mf60	97	
Ladismith	154	Ma62		www.capegardenroute.org/town_index.php?id=15
Ladybrand	155	Md60		www.go2africa.com/south-africa/eastern-highlands/ladybrand
Ladysmith	155	Me60		http://ladysmith.kzn.org.za/ls
Lake Guinas	150	Lj55		www.namibiatourism.com
Lake Liambezi	151	Mc54		www.namibiatourism.com
Lake Otjikoto	150	Lj55		www.namibiatourism.com
Lake St Lucia	155	Mg60	94f.	
Lamberts Bay	154	Lk62		www.go2africa.com
Langebaan	154	Lj62	116	www.langebaaninfo.com
Lanzerac Manor			129	
Lepokole Hills	152	Me56		www.botswana-tourism.gov.bw
Lesotho	155	Me60	108f.	
Letsibogo Dam	151	Md56		www.botswana-tourism.gov.bw
Linyanti	151	Mc55		www.botswana.co.za/africa_linyanti.html
Lisbon Falls	152	Mf58	84	www.drakensberg-tourism.com/mpumalanga-waterfalls.html
Livingstone Church	154	Mb60		www.northerncape.org.za/diamondfields/placesofinterest.html
Livingstonegrot	151	Mc58		www.africa-adventure.org/k/kodisa/
Livingstonekerk	154	Mb60		www.northerncape.org.za/diamondfields/placesofinterest.html
Livingstone's Cave	151	Mc58		www.africa-adventure.org/k/kodisa
Long Beach			123	
Long Tompas	152	Mf58		www.sabie.co.za/tour/longtom-route.html
Loskop Dam Nature Reserve	155	Me58		http://wildnetafrica.co.za/directory/client1634.html
Louis Trichardt	152	Me57		www.go2africa.com
Louwsburg	155	Mf59		www.places.co.za/html/2267.html
Lower Sabie	152	Mf58		www.parks-sa.co.za/parks/kruger/lowersabie/default.html
Lowveld			85	
Lüderitz	154	Lh59	50f.	www.namibiatourism.com
Lüderitz Bay	154	Lh59	50	
Lüderitz Shark Island Resort	154	Lh59		www.namibweb.com/luderitz.htm
Lydenburg	152	Mf58		www.lydenburg.info
Mabuasehube Game Reserve	151	Mb58		www.peaceparks.org/content/interactive/story.php?tfca=3
Machemmaruins	152	Me57		www.makhadomunicipality.co.za/tourism_places.asp
Machemma Ruins	152	Me57		www.makhadomunicipality.co.za/tourism_places.asp
Madikwe Game Reserve	151	Md58		www.southafrica-travel.net/north/a_madikwe.htm
Magoebaskloof	152	Mf57		www.go2africa.com
Mahango Game Park	151	Ma55		www.namibiatourism.com
Majuba Hill	155	Me59		www.volksrust.org.za/battleofmajuba.asp
Makgadikgadi Pans N.P.	151	Mc56	63	www.botswana-tourism.gov.bw
Makgadikgadi Salt Flats	151	Mc56	63	www.botswana-tourism.gov.bw
Malealea	155	Md60		www.go2africa.com/lesotho/lesotho/malealea/
Maletsunyane Falls	155	Me60		www.go2africa.com/lesotho/lesotho/semonkong
Malmesbury	154	Lk62		www.go2africa.com
Malolotja Nature Reserve	155	Mf59		www.sntc.org.sz/reserves/mal.html
Mamili N.P.	151	Mb55		www.namibiatourism.com
Manayana Rock Paintings	151	Mc58		www.botswana-tourism.gov.bw
Manyelanong Game Reserve	151	Mc58		www.botswana-tourism.gov.bw
Manyeleti Game Reserve	152	Mf58		www.go2africa.com
Manzini	155	Mf59		www.go2africa.com/swaziland/swaziland/manzini
Mapelane Nature Reserve	155	Mg60		www.go2africa.com
Mapungubwe	152	Me57		http://whc.unesco.org/pg.cfm?cid=31&id_site=1099
Mapungubwe (Vhembe-Dongola) N.P.	152	Me57		www.parks-sa.co.za
Marakele N.P.	151	Md58		www.parks-sa.co.za/parks/marakele/default.html
Margate	155	Mf61		www.go2africa.com/south-africa/natal-coast/margate
Mariental	150	Lj58		www.namibiatourism.com
Marloth Nature Reserve	154	Ma62		www.capenature.org.za/Nature_Reserves/html/marloth.html

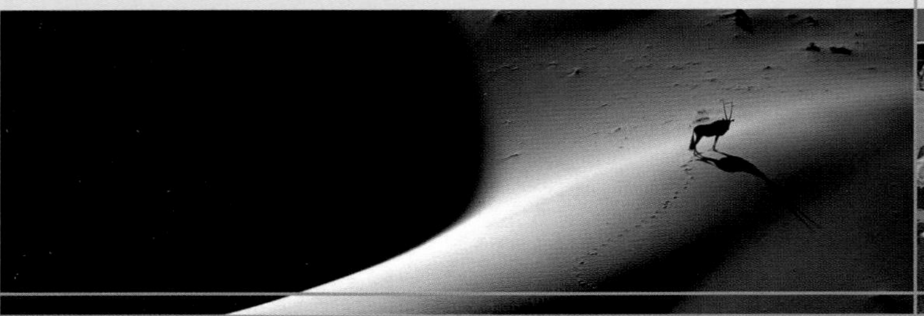

Mary Moffat's Museum	154	Mb60		www.museumsnc.co.za
Maseru	155	Md60	109	www.go2africa.com/Lesotho/Lesotho/maseru
Mashatu Game Reserve	152	Me57		www.mashatu.com
Mata Mata	151	Ma58		www.southafrica-travel.net/kalahari/e6kage01.htm
Matjiesfontein	154	Ma62		www.matjiesfontein.com
Matsieng Footprints	151	Mc58		www.botswana-tourism.gov.bw
Maun	151	Mb55		www.botswana-tourism.gov.bw/tourism/attractions/maun.html
Maun Game Sanctuary	151	Mb55		www.botswana-tourism.gov.bw/tourism/attractions/maun.html
Mazeppa Bay	155	Me62		www.places.co.za/html/mazeppa_bay.html
Mbabane	155	Mf59	91	
Mbanderu			29	
Messina	152	Mf57		www.go2africa.com/south-africa/northern-province/messina
Messum Crater	150	Lh56		www.namibiatourism.com
Middelveld			91	
Midmar Nature Reserve	155	Mf60		http://midlands.kzn.org.za/midlands/46.xml
Mineral Springs	152	Mf57		www.tourismplanet.com/pub/resort/information/6795
Miners' Memorial	154	Lj60		www.go2africa.com/south-africa/namaqualand/okiep
Mkambati Nature Reserve	155	Me61		www.ectourism.co.za
Mkhaya Nature Reserve	155	Mf59		www.go2africa.com/swaziland/swaziland/mkhaya-game-reserve
Mkuze Game Reserve	155	Mg59		www.kznwildlife.com/mkhuze_dest.htm
Mlawula Nature Reserve	155	Mf59		www.mbuluzi.co.za
Mlilwane Wildlife Sanctuary	155	Mf59		www.africantravel.com/biggameparks/mlilwane_frame.html
Modderpoort San Rock Paintings	155	Md60		www.southafrica.net/index.cfm?SitePageID=72&PlaceID=220
Mokolodi Nature Reserve	151	Mc58		www.mokolodi.com
Mokuti	150	Lj55		www.go2africa.com/accomm_temp.asp?id=2500
Molepolole	151	Mc58		www.go2africa.com/botswana/gaborone/molepolole
Mombo Camp	151	Mb55		www.eyesonafrica.net
Montagu	154	Ma62		www.southafrica-travel.net/westcape/montagu.htm
Moremi Game Reserve	151	Mb55		www.botswana-tourism.gov.bw
Moremi Gorge	151	Md57		www.botswana-tourism.gov.bw
Morija	155	Md60		www.morijafest.com
Mosselbaai	154	Mb63	137	www.mosselbay.co.za
Mossel Bay	154	Mb63	137	www.mosselbay.co.za
Motlhabaneng	152	Me56		www.botswana-tourism.gov.bw
Motloutse Ruins	152	Me57		www.tigerpawadventures.com/botswana.html
Mountain Zebra N.P.	155	Mc62		www.parks-sa.co.za/parks/mountainZebra/default.html
Mswati III., King			91	
Mudumu N.P.	151	Mb55		www.namibiatourism.com
Muizenberg	154	Lk63	122f.	www.southafrica-travel.net/westcape/cape_05.htm

N

Naboomspruit	151	Me58		www.allthehotels.net
Nahoon Reef	155	Md62		www.wannasurf.com
Namaqualand	154	Lj61	114f.	
Namaqua N.P.	154	Lj60		www.parks-sa.co.za/parks/namaqua/default.html
Namib	150	Lg55	54f.	www.go2africa.com/namibia/namib-desert
Namibia	150	Lh57	8ff.	
Namib Naukluft Park	150	Lh57	44f.	www.namibiatourism.com
Namib Rand Nature Reserve			55	
Namutoni	150	Lj55		www.namibiatourism.com
Napier	154	Lk63		www.go2africa.com/south-africa/whale-coast/napier
Nasionale Addo Olifantpark	155	Mc62		www.addoelephantpark.com
Nasionale Augrabies-watervalpark	154	Ma60		www.parks-sa.co.za/parks/augrabies_falls/default.html
Nasionale Krugerwildtuin = Kruger N.P.	152	Mf57		www.krugerpark.co.za
Nata	151	Md56		www.natalodge.com
Natal			97ff.	
Natal-Drakensberg Mountains			107	
Nata Sanctuary	151	Md56		www.botswana-tourism.gov.bw/tourism/attractions/nata.html
National West Coast Tourist Recreation Area	150	Lg56		www.namibia-travel.net/centralnamibia/skeletoncoast.htm
Naukluft	150	Lj58	44f.	www.namibian.org/travel/namibia/naukluft.htm
Naute Recreation Area	154	Lk59		www.namibian.org/travel/lodging/naute.htm
Ndumo Game Reserve	155	Mg59		www.kznwildlife.com/ndumo_dest.htm
Nelspruit	152	Mf58		www.go2africa.com/south-africa/panorama-east/nelspruit
Nilkrokodil			94	
Nodwengu	155	Mf60		http://battlefields.kzn.org.za/battlefields/about/42.html
Nongqai Fort	155	Mf60		http://goafrica.about.com/library/weekly/aa020501a.htm
Noordoewer	154	Lj60		www.namibiatourism.com
Nordhoek			123	
Norotshama River Resort	154	Lj60		www.norotshama.com
Nossob Camp ruskamp	151	Ma58		www.southafrica-travel.net/kalahari/e6kage01.htm
Ntlonyane	155	Me62		www.wannasurf.com
Ntwetwe Pan	151	Mc56		www.botswana-tourism.gov.bw
Nwanedi Game Reserve	152	Mf57		www.unep-wcmc.org/protected_areas/data/sample/0620p.htm
Nwanetsi	152	Mf58		www.singita.com
Nxai Pan	151	Mc55	63	www.botswana.co.za/africa_nxai.html
Nxai Pan N.P.	151	Mc55		www.botswana-tourism.gov.bw/tourism/attractions/nxai.html
Nylstroom	151	Me58		www.places.co.za/html/nylstroom.html
Nylsvlei Nature Reserve	152	Me58		www.places.co.za/html/nylstroom.html

O

Okahandja	150	Lj56	29	www.namibiatourism.com
Okapuka			39	
Okaukuejo	150	Lh55		http://namibia.safari.co.za/africa_okaukuejo.html
Okavango Delta	151	Mb55	64f.	www.botswana-tourism.gov.bw
Okonjima	150	Lj56		www.okonjima.com
Old Fort	154	Lj59		www.lonelyplanet.com/letters/afr/nam_pc.htm
Old wagon bridge	155	Mc60		www.thetollhouse.co.za
Olifants	152	Mf57		www.parks-sa.co.za/parks/kruger/olifants/default.html
Olifants Game Reserve	152	Mf58		www.afshowcaseprop.com/olifants.php
Olukonda National Monument	150	Lh54		www.namibia-travel.net/northnamibia/oshakati.htm
Omaruru	150	Lh56		www.namibia-travel.net/centralnamibia/omaruru.htm
Ongava Lodge	150	Lh55		http://namibia.safari.co.za/ongava-safari-lodge-namibia.html
Oog van Kuruman	154	Mb59		www.kalahari.org.za/attractions/theeye.htm
Oopmyn	155	Mc60		www.go2africa.com/south-africa/diamond-fields/kimberley
Oos-Londen	155	Md62		www.eastlondontourism.co.za
Opono Lake	150	Lh55		www.worldlakes.org/lakedetails.asp?lakeid=10507
Opuwo	150	Lg55	15	www.namibiatourism.com
Orange	154	Lj60		www.namibia-travel.net/southnamibia/orange.htm
Oranje	154	Lj60	112f.	www.namibia-travel.net/southnamibia/orange.htm
Organ Pipes	150	Lh56		www.namibiatourism.com
Otjiwarongo	150	Lj56		www.namibiatourism.com
Oudtshoorn	154	Mb62	135	www.oudtshoorn.com
Outeniqua Choo-Tjoe	154	Mb63	140f.	www.onlinesources.co.za/chootjoe
Outeniqua Mountains	154	Mb62		www.capenature.org.za/Nature_Reserves/html/outeniqua.html
Outer Pool	154	Mb63		www.wannasurf.com
Outjo	150	Lj56		www.namibiatourism.com
Ou wa-brug	155	Mc60		www.thetollhouse.co.za
Oviston Nature Reserve	155	Mc61		http://wildnetafrica.co.za/directory/client0328.html
Oxbow	155	Me60		www.go2africa.com/lesotho/lesotho/oxbow

P

Paardeberg	155	Mc60		www.civilization.ca/cwm/saw/battles/paard_e.html
Pafuri Gate	152	Mf57		www.safarinow.com/go/pafuri
Parys	155	Md59		www.go2africa.com/south-africa/vaal/parys
Paternoster	154	Lj62	116	www.southafrica-travel.net/westcape/cawc_paternoster.htm
Paul Sauer Bridge	154	Mb63		www.structurae.de/en/structures/data/s0000470/index.cfm
Petrified Dunes	150	Lh58		www.namibiatourism.com
Petrified Forest	150	Lh56		www.namibiatourism.com
Philippolis	155	Mc61		www.philippolis.org.za
Phillips Cave	150	Lh56		www.met.gov.na/central.html
Phinda Resource Reserve	155	Mg59		www.go2africa.com
Pietermaritzburg	155	Mf60	98f.	www.pietermaritzburg.co.za
Pietersburg	152	Me57		www.go2africa.com
Piet Retief	155	Mf59		www.pietretief.co.za
Piggs Peak	152	Mf58		www.mintour.gov.sz/royalexperience/casinos.html
Pilanesberg N.P.	155	Md58		www.parksnorthwest.co.za/pilanesberg
Pilgrim's Rest	152	Mf58	85	www.go2africa.com/south-africa/panorama-east/pilgrims-rest
Plettenbergbaai	154	Mb63		http://www.plettenbergbay.co.za
Plettenberg Bay	154	Mb63	143	www.plettenbergbay.co.za
Polokwane = Pietersburg	152	Me57		www.go2africa.com
Pongola Bush Nature Reserve	155	Mf59		www.zbr.co.za/nwz/pongola-bush.htm
Popa Falls	151	Ma55		www.go2africa.com/namibia/caprivi/popa-falls
Port Alfred	155	Md62		http://home.intekom.com/african_lioness/portalfred.html
Port Edward	155	Mf61		www.go2africa.com/south-africa/natal-coast/port-edward
Port Elizabeth	155	Mc62		www.pecc.gov.za
Port Saint Johns	155	Me61		www.portstjohns.org.za
Potgietersrus	151	Me58		www.places.co.za/html/mokopane.html
Prehistoric Footprints	155	Me60		www.seelesotho.com
Pretoria	151	Me58	78f.	www.pretoria.co.za
Prince Albert	154	Mb62		www.go2africa.com/south-africa/karoo/prince-albert
Punda Maria	152	Mf57		www.parks-sa.co.za/parks/kruger/pundamaria/default.html

R

Rehoboth	150	Lj57		www.namibiatourism.com
Reptielspore	152	Me57		www.safarinow.com/go/chinakalodge
Reptile Footprints	152	Me57		www.safarinow.com/go/chinakalodge
Richards Bay	155	Mg60		www.go2africa.com/south-africa/natal-safari/richards-bay
Richards Bay Nature Reserve	155	Mg60		www.go2africa.com
Richtersveld N.P.	154	Lj60		www.parks-sa.co.za/parks/Richtersveld/default.html
Robben Island	154	Lk62		http://whc.unesco.org/pg.cfm?cid=31&id_site=916
Robertson	154	Lk62		www.capetourism.org
Rock Engravings	154	Lk59		www.klausdierks.com/Chronology/1.htm
Rock Engravings	155	Mc59		www.go2africa.com/south-africa/diamond-fields/christiana
Rock Paintings	154	Ma61		www.northerncape.org.za/hantamkaroo/placesofinterest.html
Rock Paintings	155	Me61		www.seelesotho.com/travel/regions/south_west_lesotho.htm
Rorke's Drift	155	Mf60		http://battlefields.kzn.org.za/battlefields/about/29.html 19
Rössing Uranium Mine	150	Lh57		www.rossing.com
Rotsskildery	154	Ma61		www.northerncape.org.za/hantamkaroo/placesofinterest.html
Route 62	154	Lk62		www.route62.co.za
Ruacana Falls	150	Lh54		www.namibiatourism.com
Rundu	151	Lk54		www.go2africa.com/namibia/kavango/rundu
Rust de Winter Nature Reserve	152	Me58		www.sabirding.co.za/birdspot/061717.asp
Rust de Winter Nature Reserve	155	Me58		www.sabirding.co.za/birdspot/061717.asp
Rustenburg Nature Reserve	155	Md58		www.tourismnorthwest.co.za/parks/rustenburg.html

From left to right: Oryx-antelopes in the Great Namib; in Ovambo Land; the Spitzkoppe; in the Kalahari; Swakopmund.

Photo credits

Abbreviations:
C = Corbis
CE = Clemens Emmler
CH = Christian Heeb
FMF = Franz Marc Frei
IFA = IFA Bilderteam
P = Premium

Numbering from top left to bottom right. Bottom, right.

Title 1, 2, 3 CE, 2–7 CE; 7.1 Image State/Mead, 7.2 P, 7.3 FMF, 7.4 CH; 8 P; 8/9 Image State/Mead; 10.1 IFA/Fischer; 10/11 C/Johnson; 12.1 C/Arbib, 12.2 P/Plessis; 12-17 CE; 18.1 C/Gallo Images, 18.2 C/Gallo Images/Harvey, 18/19.1 Kunth, 18/19.2 P/Minden; 20 CE; 20/21 Kunth; 22.1 CE, 22.2 CE, 22.3 C/Johnson; 22–31 CE; 32.1 IFA, 32.2 CE; 32–35 CE; 36 IFA/Fischer, 36/37–45 CE: 46.1 IFA/Wolfe; 46.2-47 CE; 48.1 C/Johnson; 48/49 CE; 50.1, 2 CE, 50.3–53 CE; 54 P/Plessis, 54/55 ©Geospace EDC; 55 CE; 56 CE; 56/57 P; 58–61 CE; 62–63 P/Minden/Lanting; 64.1 CE, 64.2 P/Staebler; 64/65 IFA/Hartmann; 66.1 CE, 66.2 C/Souders; 66/67 P/Minden/Lanting; 68–69 CE; 69.1 Schapowalow; 70.1 C/Souders, 70.2 C/Harvey, 70.3 C/Gallo Images/ Dennis; 70/71 CE; 72.1 C/Svensson, 72.2 C/Ward; 72–74 CE; 74/75 FMF; 76 C/Turnley; 76/77 CE; 78.1,3 CE, 78.2 FMF; 78–81 CE; 82 FMF; 82/83–85 CE; 86.1 C/Souders, 86.2 C/Gallo Images/Reisinger, 86.3 Getty/Wolfe; 86/87 P; 87 C/Gallo Images/Dennis; 88.1, 2 C/Gullin, 88.3 C/Allofs, 88.4 C/Johnson, 88.5 C/Gallo Images, 88.6, 7 C/Harvey, 88.8 C/Gallo Images/ Haagener; 88/89 C/Gallo Images/Dennis; 90.1 CE, 90.2 C/Frank Lane Picture Agency/Perry, 90.3 C/Johnson; 90/91 CE; 92 C/Harvey; 92/93 C/Davis; 93 CE; 94 C/Gallo Images/Dennis; 94/95 laif/Riehle; 96–101 CE; 102–103 FMF; 104 C/Rotmann; 104/105 P/Pacific Stock/Watt; 106.1, 2 CE, 106.3 IFA/Aberham; 106/107-109 CE; 110.1, 2, 3, 4 C Sygma/Herve, 110.5, 6 C/O´Rear; 110/111 C Sygma/Herve; 112 FMF; 112/113–115 CE; 116.1 C/Gallo Images/ Bannister, 116.2-119 CE; 120.1 IFA/John Arnold Images, 120.2– 122.3 CE; 122/123 C/Houser; 123–132.5 CE; 132.6 C/Blair; 132/133.1 CE; 132/133.2 IFA/John Arnold Images; 134.1 IFA/Sohns, 134.2 CE; 134/135–138 CE; 138/139 FMF; 140 afripics/L. Von Horsten; 140/141 Das Fotoarchiv; 142–143 CE; 144.1, 2 C/Gallo Images/ Dennis; 144/145 C/Souders; 146–147 CH; 148/149 CE; 156.1 C/Souders, 156.2 CE; 157.1 C/Houser, 157.2 C/Gallo Imagges; 158.1 P, 158.2–159 CE.

This edition is published on behalf of APA Publications GmbH & Co. Verlag KG, Singapore Branch, Singapore by Verlag Wolfgang Kunth GmbH & Co KG, Munich, Germany

Distribution of this edition:

GeoCenter International Ltd
Meridian House, Churchill Way West
Basingstoke, Hampshire RG21 6YR
Great Britain
Tel.: (44) 1256 817 987
Fax: (44) 1256 817 988
sales@geocenter.co.uk
www.insightguides.com

ISBN 978-981-258-869-2

Original edition:
© 2007 Verlag Wolfgang Kunth GmbH & Co. KG, Munich
Königinstr. 11
80539 Munich
Ph: +49.89.45 80 20-0
Fax: +49.89.45 80 20-21
www.kunth-verlag.de

English edition:

Text: Daniela Schetar
Translation: Robert Strain, JMS Books LLP

Printed in Slovakia